Games to Play with Toddlers
Revised

Jackie Silberg

Illustrated by Joan Waites

Author Availability

Jackie Silberg is an acclaimed speaker, teacher, and trainer on early childhood development and music. You can arrange to have her speak, present, train, or entertain by contacting her through Gryphon House, PO Box 207, Beltsville MD 20704-0207 or at jsilberg@interserv.com.

Other Books by Jackie Silberg

Games to Play with Babies, Third Edition
Games to Play with Two-Year-Olds, Revised
125 Brain Games for Babies
125 Brain Games for Toddlers and Twos
300 Three Minute Games
500 Five Minute Games
The I Can't Sing Book
The Complete Book of Rhymes, Songs, Poems,
Fingerplays, and Chants, wth Pam Schiller

Bulk Purchase

Gryphon House books are available at special discount for special premiums and sales promotions as well as for fund-raising use. Special editions or book excerpts also can be created to specification. For details, contact the Director of Sales at Gryphon House.

Jackie Silberg
Games to Play with Toddlers

Over 50 New Games!

Illustrated by Joan Waites

gryphon house®, inc.
Beltsville, MD 20704

Revised

Dedication

This book is dedicated to the joy that toddlers bring into our lives.

Acknowledgments

Thanks to Kathy Charner, the most wonderful editor an author can have.
She makes the words come alive. And to the Gryphon House family who work
together to produce the beautiful product that you are looking at now.

Copyright

Copyright © 2002 Jackie Silberg
Published by Gryphon House, Inc.
10726 Tucker Street, Beltsville, MD 20705
Visit us on the web at www.gryphonhouse.com
Illustrations: Joan Waites
Cover photograph: © Artville, LLC., 1999

Library of Congress Cataloging-in-Publication Data

Silberg, Jackie, 1934–
    Games to play with toddlers / Jackie Silberg; illustrated by Joan Waites.--
    Rev. p. cm.
    Includes index.
    ISBN 0-87659-234-5
    1. Games. 2. Educational games. 3. Toddlers. I. Title.

GV1203 .S537 2002
649'.5--dc21

2002019788

Disclaimer

The publisher and the author cannot be held responsible for injury, mishap, or
damages incurred during the use of or because of the activities in this book.
The author recommends appropriate and reasonable supervision at all times
based on the age and capability of each child.

Table of Contents

Games for 15- to 18-month-olds

Games for 18- to 21-month-olds

Games for 21- to 24-month-olds

From the Author

What is more precious than a toddler exploring the world, dropping food on the floor to see if it will bounce, running from here to there, or listening to the same story or song hundreds of times? Toddlers learn from all of these experiences. When a child plays, she is developing listening, language, cognitive, motor, social, and self-esteem skills that are critical to her development.

This book contains fresh, innovative, and stimulating games for you and your child to play and grow together. Whether it's building with blocks, whispering at quiet times, playing with toys, or laughing together, you will find terrific ideas to enjoy with your child and help him learn.

The carefully selected games in this book have been played and enjoyed by adults and toddlers for many years. Originating from a variety of cultures and ethnic backgrounds, the games were carefully selected for each age range.

Enjoy them all!

Jackie Silberg

Age Range

The age range given for each activity is an approximation. Each child develops at his or her own pace. Use your knowledge of each individual child as the best judgment as to whether an activity is appropriate.

Guidelines for Growth

While each child's development will be individual and unique, the following skills are those that toddlers will likely develop before age two.

Motor, Auditory, and Visual Skills
Walks independently
Walks up and down stairs holding an adult's hand
Holds two small objects in one hand
Jumps in place
Kicks a large ball
Throws a small ball overhand
Recognizes familiar people
Scribbles on paper
Stacks three to six blocks
Turns knobs
Finds objects of the same color, shape, and size
Points to distant, interesting objects outdoors
Turns toward a family member whose name is spoken
Understands and follows a simple direction
Notices sounds made by a clock, bell, and whistle
Responds rhythmically to music with her whole body
Carries out instructions that include two steps

Language and Cognitive Skills
Jabbers with expression
Identifies pictures in a book
Uses single words meaningfully
Names objects when asked, "What's this?"
Uses 20 or more words
Names at least 25 familiar objects
Gestures to make his wants known
Names toys
Uses words to make her wants known
Combines two different words
Tries to sing

Speaks in simple sentences
Finds familiar objects
Fits objects into containers
Turns two to three pages of a book at a time
Points to pictures in a book
Remembers where objects belong
Obtains a toy using a stick or a string

Self-Concept Skills
Demands personal attention
Points to parts of his body when identified
Insists on helping to feed herself
Names parts of a doll's body
Claims objects as his own
Refers to herself by name
Pulls on socks and mittens
Eats with a spoon
Drinks from a cup
Attempts to wash himself
Offers a toy but does not release it
Plays independently around another child
Enjoys short walks
Asks for food and water when needed

12-15 months

Color Games

- The first step in learning to identify colors is matching them.

- Sit on the floor with your child. Zoom a toy car back and forth. Choose a red or blue car.

- After you and your toddler have played a while, take out a car of a different color and play with that one.

- Next, take two sheets of paper the same color as the cars. Put the paper on the floor and the cars on the matching paper.

- Take a car off the paper and ask your child to put the car on the matching paper. As you play this game, always name the color to which you are referring.

- Consistently playing this game will develop your child's matching skills.

Color Fun

- Find two small containers that are the same size. Margarine tubs work nicely.

- Paint or color one red and the other yellow. If you can find containers in these colors that is even better.

- Put the containers in front of your child. Touch each container and say the color name.

- Take your child's hand and touch each container as you say the name again.

- Pick up the yellow container and say, "I like the yellow one."

- Ask your child, "Would you like the yellow one?" Give the container to your child.

- Continue taking a container and then giving it to your child.

- Put a small object in the yellow container. Hold up each container and shake it. Your child will enjoy the noise.

- Ask your child to give you the yellow container.

- After you play this game a few times, your child will be able recognize the noisy container by the color.

Color Walk

- Go on a color walk to bond with your toddler. Select a toy of a certain color to bring with you.

- Find one or two objects in each room that are the same color as the toy.

- Talk about what you've found, for example, "Daddy's yellow tie is the same color as your yellow ball," or "Mommy's blue blouse is the same color as your blue block."

- A variation of this game is to carry a laundry basket around, collecting toys and other objects of the same color.

Cha, Cha, Cha

- Place marbles or other objects that make interesting sounds inside a metal tin.

- Tape the lid securely, making sure there are no sharp edges.

- Give the tin to your toddler and encourage her to shake it while you sing with her.

- Sing a familiar tune such as "Old MacDonald Had a Farm."

- Next, in a sing-song voice, sing the words, "One, two, cha, cha, cha."

- Show your child how to shake the tin on "cha, cha, cha."

- Repeat several times. Soon your toddler will understand to shake the tin on "cha, cha, cha."

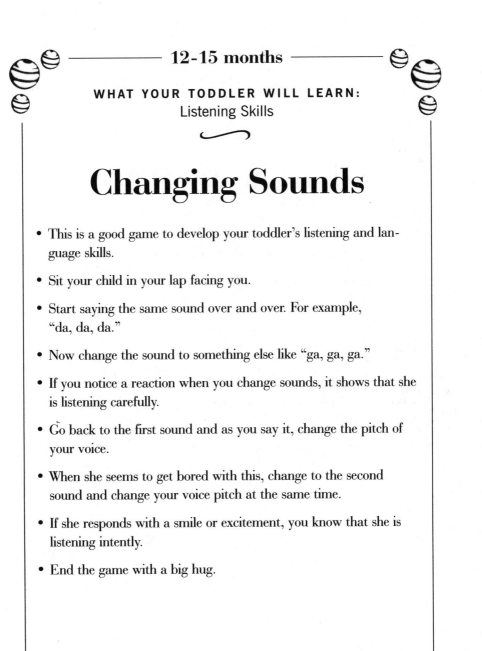

WHAT YOUR TODDLER WILL LEARN:
Listening Skills

Changing Sounds

- This is a good game to develop your toddler's listening and language skills.

- Sit your child in your lap facing you.

- Start saying the same sound over and over. For example, "da, da, da."

- Now change the sound to something else like "ga, ga, ga."

- If you notice a reaction when you change sounds, it shows that she is listening carefully.

- Go back to the first sound and as you say it, change the pitch of your voice.

- When she seems to get bored with this, change to the second sound and change your voice pitch at the same time.

- If she responds with a smile or excitement, you know that she is listening intently.

- End the game with a big hug.

Sounds Are Fun

- Look at your toddler and make vowel sounds. Say each vowel several times and then stop and see if your child will copy you.

- Say the vowel sounds in different pitches. Say them high and say them low. Say them fast and say them slowly.

- Combine two vowel sounds, for example "ee, ee, ee, ah, ah, ah."

- Make up melodies to go with the vowel sounds.

- The more that you play with sounds, the more your child will enjoy the sounds that he makes, too.

- This is a beginning step in developing a positive attitude about words and eventually reading.

WHAT YOUR TODDLER WILL LEARN:
About Animals

Animal Sounds

- Toddlers really enjoy making animal sounds.

- Gather plastic toy animals. Show your toddler an animal and tell her the sound that it makes.

- Ask her to copy you and make the animal sound, too.

- Show your child a picture and ask her to find the matching toy and make its sound.

- Look through magazines with your child to find pictures of familiar animals. Cut them out and put them on cardboard to make your own animal book.

"Baah"

Dressing Talk

- When children are starting to talk, echo the sounds that they make.

- By changing the inflection and intensity of your voice, you stimulate their language development.

- While dressing your toddler, talk about what you are doing in simple two- or three-word sentences.

- For example, while changing her diaper, say things such as, "change, change, change" or "diaper off, diaper on."

- Change the rhythm of your words. For example, you can say, "ma, ma, ma, ma, I love you," rapidly or slowly, or create a rhythm that is syncopated or alternates fast and slow, loud and soft.

- By repeating your toddler's language and adding a word or two of your own, you help her develop language skills.

The Patting Game

- This game develops hearing and feeling connections for rhythm.

- Hold your toddler on your lap.

- Say the words to a familiar poem or nursery rhyme.

- As you say the words, gently pat your child to the rhythm of the words. You can pat her on the back, on the shoulder, or on the leg.

- Take your child's hand and let her pat you on the shoulder.

- You can change the tempo of the words and pat at different speeds.

- This game can also be played with recorded music.

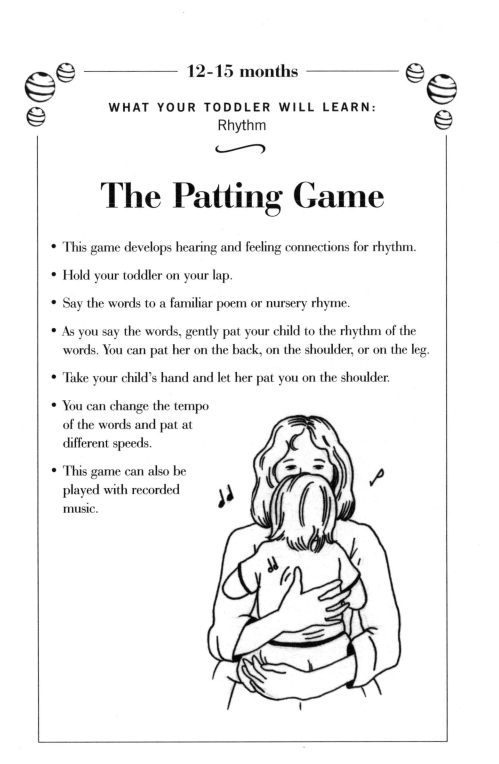

Games to Play with Toddlers

Smells

- Your toddler had a fully developed sense of smell at birth. You may have memories associated with smells.

- Play a smell game with your child. Think of several objects with easily identifiable smells, such as flowers or grass.

- The kitchen is full of wonderful odors, especially spices.

- Say to your child, "Let's smell the flowers." Hold a flower up to her nose and show her how to smell it.

- Respond to the smell with, "Oh, that smells wonderful."

- After you have smelled two things (for example, cinnamon and flowers), put a flower and some cinnamon on a table. Ask your child to point to the flower. Help her point if she doesn't know how and then smell it together.

- Repeat the same thing with the cinnamon.

- Take advantage of the seasons to smell things outdoors.

WHAT YOUR TODDLER WILL LEARN:
Imagination

Tubes and More

- Show your child the different things that you can do with a paper towel tube.

- Pretend it's a microphone.

- Pretend that it's a baton and lead the band.

- Hold it to your eye and pretend it's a telescope.

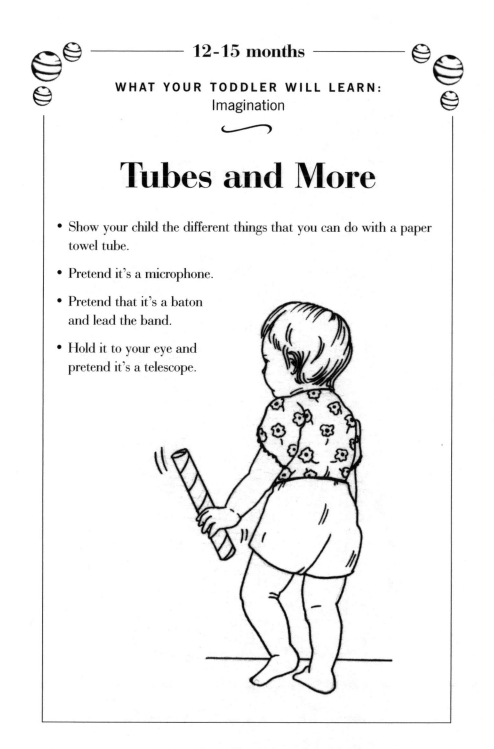

Teddy Bear Train

- Find several boxes large enough to hold a teddy bear or another stuffed animal.

- Hook the boxes together with strong tape or rope.

- Ask the teddy bear if he would like to go for a train ride.

- Ask your toddler to put the teddy into a box.

- Ask your toddler if she wants any of the other animals to go for a ride.

- Give the rope to your toddler and see if she can pull the train.

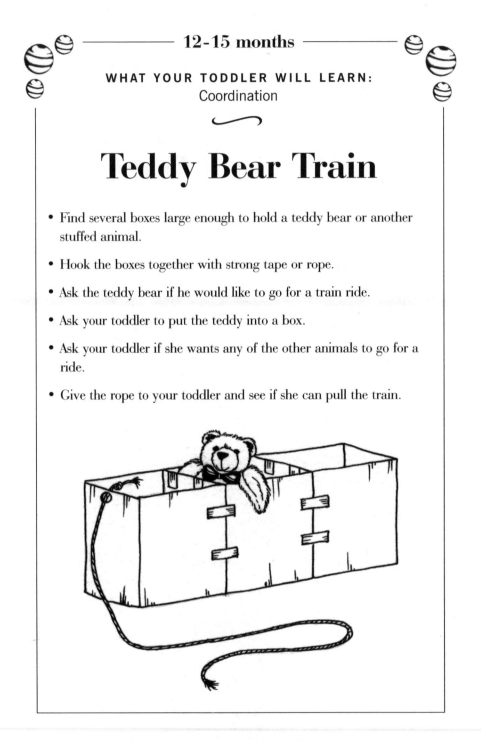

The In and Out Game

- Find a box with individual compartments. When buying things by the case, you often get this kind of box.

- Save paper towel tubes or plastic bottles.

- Give your child the tubes or bottles to put into the compartments and then take them out again.

- Ask her to put the tube "in" the box and then take it "out."

- Toddlers will do this happily for long periods.

WHAT YOUR TODDLER WILL LEARN:
Creativity

Paper Sack Blocks

- You will need several small paper grocery sacks and lots of newspaper.

- Ask your toddler to help you crumple the newspaper and stuff it into paper sacks.

- When all the sacks are full, close them tightly with tape or string.

- These sacks are now lightweight blocks that are easy for your toddler to move around.

- Experiment with your child and show her different things to do with the paper sack blocks:
    - Stack the blocks.
    - Lay them side by side.
    - Put them in a circle.
    - Throw one back and forth.
    - Try drawing faces on the sacks to turn them into puppets.

Boom, Boom, Down

- Toddlers adore piling up blocks and knocking them down.

- Help your child build a tower of blocks. Three or four is about all a toddler can stack because she can hardly refrain from knocking them over.

- When the blocks are stacked, say, "One and a two and a boom, boom, down!"

- On the word "down," knock down the blocks.

- After you have played this a few times, try stacking the blocks higher.

More Block Games

- Plastic bowls in different sizes are good beginning blocks because they are easy to manipulate and lightweight.

- Toddlers will enjoy trying to nest them in each other.

- You can also put the lids on the bowls and encourage your toddler to try stacking them.

- Through trial and error your child will soon learn that the bigger bowls go on the bottom.

- Trying to take the lids off the bowls and putting the lids back on the bowls will be a great challenge to your child.

- While you are playing with your child, talk about concepts such as numbers—one bowl, two bowls, and so on.

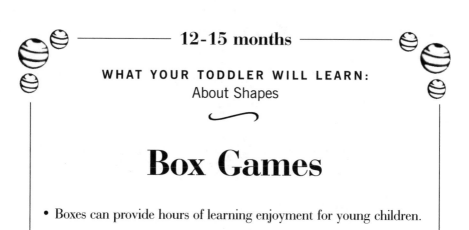

Box Games

- Boxes can provide hours of learning enjoyment for young children.

- Gather several small toys and plastic containers. Give your child a large box. Encourage her to drop the toys into the box and dump them out again.

- Cut out shapes (circles, squares, triangles) from the top of a box. Give your toddler the shapes and see if she can fit them into the correct holes.

- Give your toddler several boxes of different sizes. Help her learn how to stack the boxes. She will soon understand to put the largest on the bottom. The same boxes can be used for nesting.

WHAT YOUR TODDLER WILL LEARN:
Fine Motor Skills

Dump the Balls

- Place soft balls or other small soft objects in a box.

- Dump all of the balls out of the box.

- Encourage your child to pick up the balls one at a time and put them back into the box.

- Dump the balls out again and ask your child to pick them up.

- After you have played this game a few times, start dumping the balls out in different ways. For example, take them out one by one or tip the box over with your foot.

- Your child will quickly scramble to put the balls back into the box.

- Toddlers are absolutely delighted with this game and will soon be playing the game themselves.

WHAT YOUR TODDLER WILL LEARN:
Balance

Beach Ball Fun

- Get a large and colorful beach ball.

- Roll the ball to your toddler.

- Take a stuffed animal and put it on top of the ball.

- Roll the ball back and forth holding onto the toy.

- Ask your child if she would like to sit on the ball.

- If your toddler agrees, hold her securely while balancing her on the ball.

- As you roll the ball in different directions, say the corresponding words, "back and forth," "side to side," and "left and right."

WHAT YOUR TODDLER WILL LEARN:
Exploration Skills

What's in the Drawer?

- Curiosity is the backbone of a child's development of competence. From your child's earliest perceptions onward, she will want to feel and explore everything and experience the world through all of her senses.

- In a small, easily opened drawer in the kitchen, place many different objects, such as plastic containers, pans, and wooden spoons.

- Place anything in the drawer that has no sharp edges and is safe for your child to play with.

- Leave the drawer ajar while you are in the kitchen, and you will have a happy, curious companion bent on exploring her drawer.

- From time to time, change the contents of the drawer.

  NOTE: Safety latches are a must for other drawers and cabinet doors in the kitchen.

WHAT YOUR TODDLER WILL LEARN:
Observation Skills

Spin Around

- You will need a lazy Susan (kitchen turntable) for this game.

- Young children love to spin these turntables and are happy just watching them spin.

- Place a small object on the turntable and spin it around. Observe what happens to it.

- Tape a small toy to the turntable. Tell your child that you are going to give it a ride.

WHAT YOUR TODDLER WILL LEARN:
Coordination

Clip the Clothespin

- Remove the lid from a large can or similar container that has no sharp or ragged metal edges.

- Show your toddler how to slip an old-fashioned wooden "doll" clothespin (without metal springs) onto the rim of the can.

- Give your child several clothespins to put on the can, and then show her how to drop the clothespins into the can.

- Toddlers are fascinated with this game, which is excellent for eye-hand coordination.

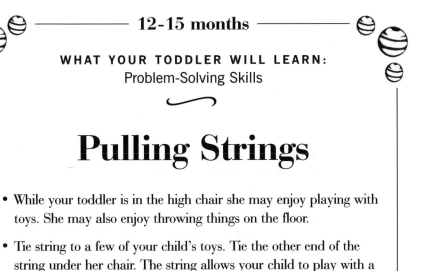

WHAT YOUR TODDLER WILL LEARN:
Problem-Solving Skills

Pulling Strings

- While your toddler is in the high chair she may enjoy playing with toys. She may also enjoy throwing things on the floor.

- Tie string to a few of your child's toys. Tie the other end of the string under her chair. The string allows your child to play with a toy without its falling to the floor.

  NOTE: Be sure the string is not long enough to pose a choking hazard.

- Your toddler also will find it a challenge to pull the strings to retrieve the toys.

WHAT YOUR TODDLER WILL LEARN:
Toys Are Fun

Toys for Toddlers

- When selecting toys, look for toys that:
    - Stimulate eye-hand coordination
    - Allow your toddler to be active and do something
    - Teach cause and effect
    - Are safe
    - Are sturdy
    - Stimulate imagination

- Some suggestions are unbreakable mirrors, squeeze toys, rhythm sticks, drums, toy pianos, playdough, and simple puzzles.

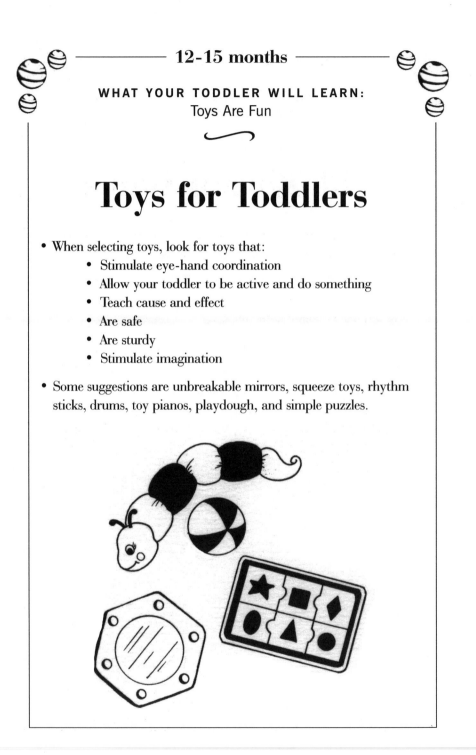

The Tearing Game

- Toddlers really enjoy tearing things. This is a good game to play in the kitchen where you can supervise your toddler closely.

- Collect old magazines, tissue paper, wrapping paper, and foil. Each provides an interesting tearing experience because the textures and sounds differ.

- Show your child how to tear the paper and drop it into a box. Because toddlers like to put things in their mouths, keep a close watch.

- Wad a piece of paper into a ball and throw it. Show your child how to do this. If she cannot make the ball, do it for her and give it to her to throw.

WHAT YOUR TODDLER WILL LEARN:
Problem-Solving Skills

Cereal Fun

- Seat your toddler in her high chair.

- Drop a small piece of dry cereal into a small-mouthed bottle.

- Your toddler must figure out that she cannot reach inside to get the cereal and will have to tip the bottle.

- Once your child figures this out, the next step is for her to put the cereal into the bottle and then remove it.

Puzzle Fun

- Select cookie cutters that your child recognizes and enjoys.

- Press a cookie cutter into a piece of Styrofoam. Use a separate piece of Styrofoam for each cookie cutter.

- Carefully cut around the outline and remove the cutout, keeping the Styrofoam frame intact. Give the cutout to your toddler and show her how to fit it back into the Styrofoam.

- Put the pieces and cutouts on a table and watch your child concentrate deeply as she matches them.

- Once your toddler easily matches all the cutouts, try making several cutouts in a larger piece of Styrofoam.

Scribbling Game

- Giving your toddler plenty of crayons, markers, pencils, and chalk will encourage him to scribble. Scribbling develops eye-hand coordination, which is important in a young child's development.

- Supervised scribbling can be great fun for you and your child.

- Sit at a table with your toddler. Spread drawing paper on the table. Show her how to place the crayon on the paper and move her hand back and forth.

- Praise the lines and squiggles that she makes, noting a specific feature. For example, "I really like the round red lines in your picture."

- If your toddler appears reluctant or unsure about drawing, draw an interesting shape and say, "I made a picture. Can you make a picture?"

- Games like these develop your toddler's self-esteem.

WHAT YOUR TODDLER WILL LEARN:
Balance

Spin Around

• Spinning around with your toddler is always great fun, especially if you are holding her in your arms as you spin.

• Spin for short periods of time so that neither of you gets dizzy.

• Hold your child in your arms in a rocking motion or upright with her head over one of your shoulders.

• Sing as you spin. Any song that you choose will be just fine.

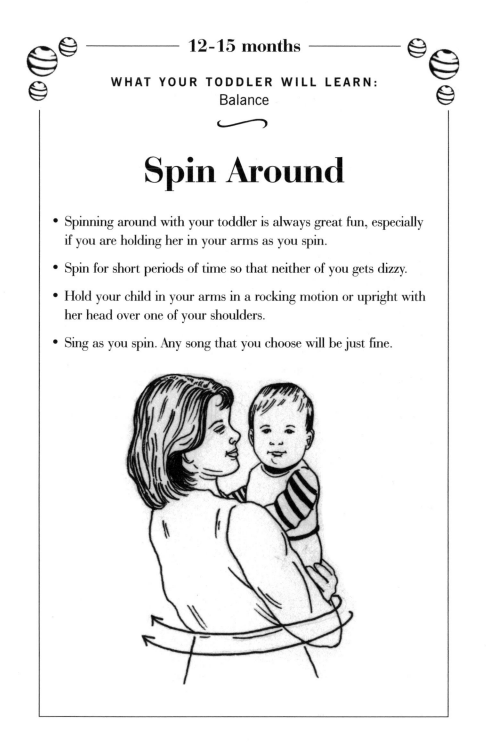

WHAT YOUR TODDLER WILL LEARN:
Fun

Peekaboo Box

- You will need a box large enough for your toddler to crawl inside.

- Cut a hole large enough for your child to put her head through.

- Encourage your toddler to crawl into the box.

- Play peekaboo with you on the outside and your child on the inside. Either you or your toddler can put your head into the hole and say, "Peekaboo!"

- Build anticipation by saying, "One, two, three...peekaboo!"

- When you put your head in the hole, change the way you look. Make a funny face, put a scarf on your head or around your neck, or put on a pair of glasses. This makes the game even more fun for your child.

The Tunnel

- Use boxes, pillows, and sheets to make a tunnel.

- Show your toddler how to crawl through the tunnel.

- Tell her, "Let's crawl into the tunnel."

- Start crawling and encourage her to follow you.

- As you are crawling, say, "We are inside the tunnel."

- When you get to the other end, say, "Now we are outside the tunnel."

- Go back into the tunnel and say, "Now we are inside the tunnel."

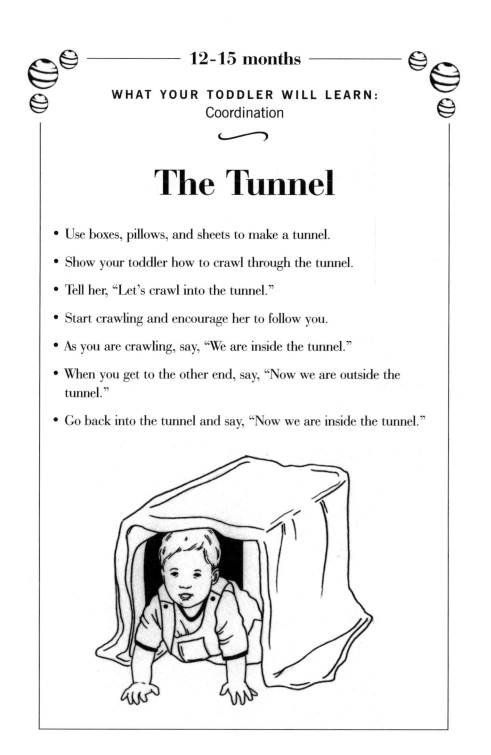

WHAT YOUR TODDLER WILL LEARN:
Coordination

Crawl a Little, Walk a Little

- When toddlers first start walking, they still enjoy crawling because it gets them to their destination faster.

- Playing a crawling-walking game will help your toddler to practice walking and still give her the opportunity to crawl if she so desires.

- Pick a favorite song that your toddler enjoys. Some popular ones are "Twinkle, Twinkle, Little Star," "The Eensy Weensy Spider," and "The ABC Song."

- Start singing and walking to the song. It's best to hold your toddler's hand as you do this. At the end of the first verse, change to crawling as you sing. Switch between walking and crawling several times during the song.

- Your little one will probably want to change often, as this game is great fun.

WHAT YOUR TODDLER WILL LEARN:
About Opposites

Hot and Cold

- Sit in a chair with your toddler on your lap facing you.

- Say, "I'm so-o-o-o hot," and lift the child up into your arms.

- Say, "I'm so-o-o-o cold," and open your legs. Ease the child down to the floor while you hold her firmly.

- After a few times, ask the child whether she wants hot or cold. Act out whichever she selects.

- After your toddler has learned this game, suggest that she play it with a stuffed animal.

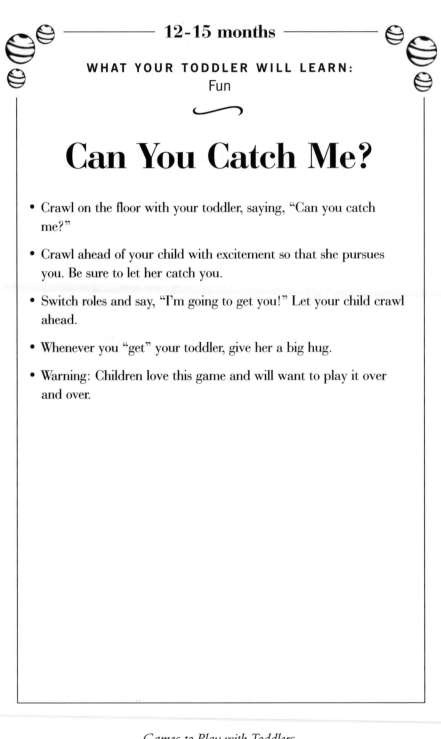

WHAT YOUR TODDLER WILL LEARN:
Fun

Can You Catch Me?

- Crawl on the floor with your toddler, saying, "Can you catch me?"

- Crawl ahead of your child with excitement so that she pursues you. Be sure to let her catch you.

- Switch roles and say, "I'm going to get you!" Let your child crawl ahead.

- Whenever you "get" your toddler, give her a big hug.

- Warning: Children love this game and will want to play it over and over.

WHAT YOUR TODDLER WILL LEARN:
Language Skills

Where's the Chick?

- Hide behind a door and say, "Cheep, cheep, cheep."

- Ask your toddler to find the baby chick.

- If she has trouble, stick out your head or foot so that she can see you.

- Hide somewhere different and play the game again.

- Change the animal to a baby cow, baby duck, or other baby animal. Each time, make the sounds appropriate to that animal.

- After a few times, your child will want to hide and make the animal sounds herself.

Where Is It?

- Play this game in one room.

- Walk around the room with your toddler, naming objects. Speak in short, clear sentences.
    - This is a chair.
    - This is a table.
    - This is the door.

- Then ask your toddler, "Where is the chair?"

- Continue asking about each object that you named.

WHAT YOUR TODDLER WILL LEARN:
Bonding

Peekaboo

- Play "Peekaboo" with your child many different ways.

- Cover your eyes with your hands.

- Place the child's hands over her eyes.

- Hang a blanket between you and your child. Peek out at the side, top and bottom of the blanket.

- Peek around a large toy, doll, washcloth, or towel.

- Lay your toddler on the bed. Toss a lightweight blanket over her body and lift it up and down as you peek under.

Touch the Toy

- Put a familiar toy in a box. A shoebox is good to use with this game.

- Make a hole in the top of the box large enough for your hand to fit inside.

- Ask your toddler to put her hand in the box and feel the toy.

- Now, put your hand in the box and feel the toy.

- Repeat this several times so that your toddler has a chance to experience the toy by feel.

- Take the toy out of the box and put it on the floor next to another toy.

- Your child may be able to identify which toy was in the box because even though she couldn't see the toy in the box, she may recognize it by the way it feels.

WHAT YOUR TODDLER WILL LEARN:
About Following Directions

Doll Play

- This is a wonderful kitchen game to play while waiting for a meal.

- Give your child her favorite doll or stuffed animal. Ask her about it: "Is [name of doll] hungry? Is he sleepy?"

- Direct your child to do things with her doll.
    - Give your doll a kiss.
    - Hug your baby.
    - Rock your baby.
    - Give your doll some milk.
    - Can you give your baby a bath?
    - Change your baby's diaper.

- All these directions will elicit some response from your toddler. As she begins to enjoy the directions, her listening skills will become more acute.

WHAT YOUR TODDLER WILL LEARN:
Concentration

Where's the Bear?

- Tie one end of a long string around your child's favorite teddy bear and hide the bear in a closet.

- Close the closet door, trail the string out under the door and run it around the room, over and under furniture and other objects.

- Say to your toddler, "Let's find Teddy."

- Help her hold the string and follow it to the bear.

- Your child will absolutely love this game. Play it again, and as you follow the string, describe where you are going. For example, "The string is behind the chair," "The string is under the rug," and so on.

- When you find the teddy bear, give him a big hug and say, "Oh, Teddy, we're so glad we found you!"

WHAT YOUR TODDLER WILL LEARN:
Play Skills

Pretending

- Use a teddy bear to help your toddler learn new tasks.

- Talk to the teddy bear and to your child. For example, "Annie, would you like to drink from the cup?" "Teddy, would you like to drink from the cup?" Pretend to give teddy a drink.

- There are many things that you can do with teddy and your child together.
  - Rock teddy in your arms.
  - Give teddy a kiss.
  - Hold teddy high in the air.
  - Tickle teddy on the tummy.
  - Ask teddy to wave "bye-bye."

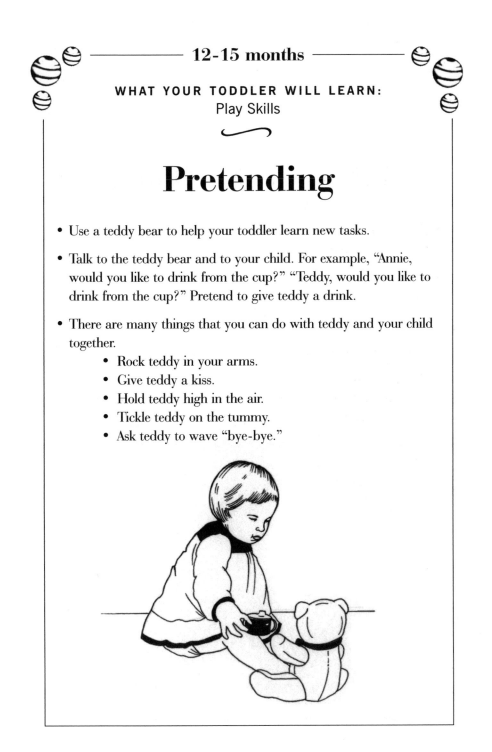

Games to Play with Toddlers

The Touching Game

• Playing a touch-and-name game will help your toddler learn more about herself.

• Recite this rhyme with your child.

> *Can you touch your head?*
> *Can you touch your head?*
> *One, two, three,*
> *Can you touch your head?*

• Repeat the rhyme, naming a different part of the body each time.

• After you feel sure that your toddler knows at least three or four parts well, give her a teddy bear and ask her to touch the same parts on the bear.

• If she can play this game with the bear, it means that she has understood and acquired the concepts.

Body Part Game

- When a young child is beginning to name the parts of her body, play this game.

- Touch your ears, saying to the child, "I am touching my ears. Can you touch your ears?"

- Give your toddler time and repeat the question if needed. If she is keeping up, use words that she doesn't usually hear, such as elbows, chin, ankles, back, and so on. Encourage her to say the words, too.

- If your child touches a new part of her body, name that part as you imitate her.

- Songs that name parts of the body will reinforce this game, such as "Looby Loo" and "Hokey Pokey."

Blowing

- Sit your toddler in your lap and touch her lips. As you touch her lips, say the word "lips."

- Take your child's fingers and put them on your lips and say the words, "[your name's] lips."

- Use your lips to blow a stream of air on your toddler's palm.

- Put some torn up tissue paper on a table and show your toddler how you can blow it around.

- Encourage your child to copy you and to blow.

- Play a game of counting. "One, two, three, blow."

WHAT YOUR TODDLER WILL LEARN:
About Following Directions

Washing Fun

- Water and young children are definitely attracted to one another.

- Fill a bucket or large pan with water.

- Give your child a washcloth or small sponge, plastic dinnerware, old silverware, and anything else that she can pretend to wash.

- While you are outside, there are many other things that she could try to wash, such as tables, chairs, or several rocks of different shapes and sizes. Observe that many rocks change their color and texture when washed.

NOTE: Supervise closely.

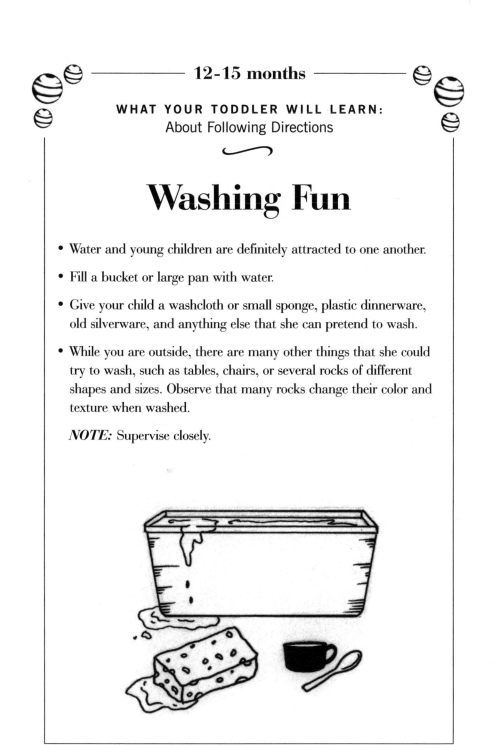

Happy Feet

- Walking on a variety of surfaces helps young children develop good eye-foot coordination.

- Walk barefoot on smooth pebbles. Talk about how your feet feel. Walk barefoot in sand. Notice that you have to carry your body differently on pebbles than on sand.

- While barefoot, try walking on pillows, logs, grass, cement, bricks, and other surfaces.

- Each time that you vary the surface, you adjust your body, which develops eye-foot coordination.

WHAT YOUR TODDLER WILL LEARN:
Nature Appreciation

Outdoor Fun

- Take your toddler outside and discover all kinds of wonderful things.
    - Feel the wind in your hair.
    - Feel the raindrops on your face.
    - Smell a flower.
    - Watch a butterfly.
    - Hold a worm in your hands.
    - Lie in the grass and look at the clouds.
    - Squish your toes in the mud.

- More things to do:
    - Crunch an autumn leaf.
    - Jump in a pile of leaves.
    - Care for plants and watch them grow.
    - Taste fresh fruits and vegetables from the garden.
    - Taste a snowflake.

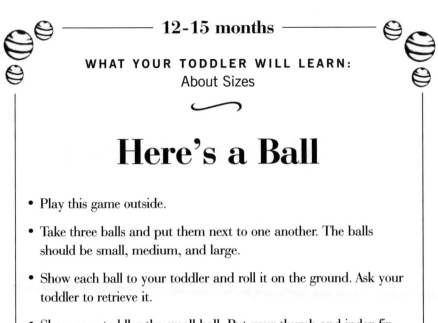

WHAT YOUR TODDLER WILL LEARN:
About Sizes

Here's a Ball

- Play this game outside.

- Take three balls and put them next to one another. The balls should be small, medium, and large.

- Show each ball to your toddler and roll it on the ground. Ask your toddler to retrieve it.

- Show your toddler the small ball. Put your thumb and index finger together to make a circle. Say to your toddler, "Just like the small ball."

- Show your toddler the medium ball. Put your two thumbs together and your two index fingers together to make a circle and say, "Just like the bigger ball."

- Show your toddler the large ball. Put your hands together over your head to make a big ball. Say, "Just like the biggest ball."

- Roll each ball to your toddler again. Ask her to retrieve each one.

Neighborhood Visit

- Toddlers adore this game. It not only develops their language, but helps them become familiar with their surroundings.

- Take your toddler for a walk around the neighborhood. As you pass interesting things, stop and talk to them.

- Talk to the flowers, the bugs, the grass, and so forth, saying something like: "Hello, grass. My name is Susie. We are taking a walk around the neighborhood. Bye-bye."

- Repeat the sequence each time you decide to talk to something.

15-18 months

WHAT YOUR TODDLER WILL LEARN:
Fine Motor Skills

Cup Stacking

- Gather several small paper cups.

- Put them together and then take them apart as your toddler watches.

- Your child will want to do the same.

- After he has done this several times, add other cups of different shapes or sizes.

- Watch how he experiments to see which cups fit into other cups.

- This is a lovely game that develops problem-solving and thinking skills.

WHAT YOUR TODDLER WILL LEARN:
Coordination

Building Blocks

- Sit on the floor with your toddler.

- Put down one block and say, "I am putting one block on the floor."

- Add a block and say, "I am putting two blocks on the floor."

- Repeat with a third block.

- Knock down the tower. Urge the child to rebuild it, with your help, if necessary.

- As the child's coordination increases, the tower will get taller.

WHAT YOUR TODDLER WILL LEARN:
Fine Motor Skills

Disposable Blocks

- Make disposable blocks out of small milk cartons.

- Tape all of the ends together and cover the cartons with contact paper.

- Let your toddler decorate the blocks with crayons or stickers.

- Play a stacking game with your toddler. Praise him each time he stacks one block on top of another.

- The most fun is to knock down the stacks.

- The great thing about these blocks is that you can throw them away when your child is no longer interested in playing with them.

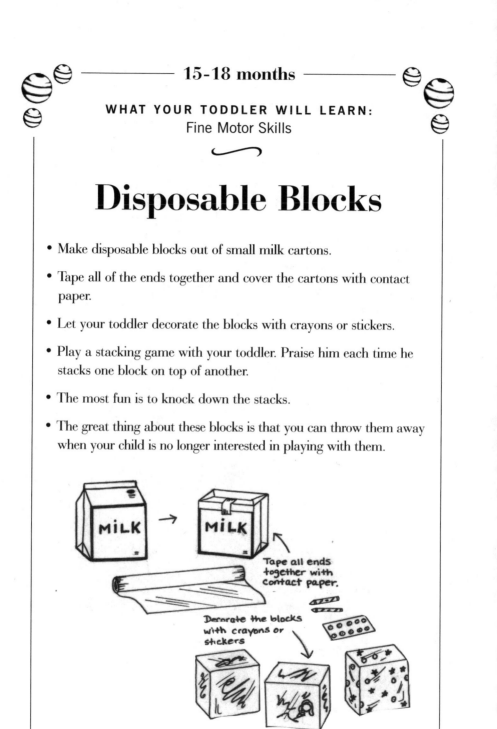

Tape all ends together with contact paper.

Decorate the blocks with crayons or stickers

WHAT YOUR TODDLER WILL LEARN:
Creativity

Beanbag Fun

- Beanbags are excellent toys for young children. They are safe, soft, and they stimulate creativity.

- Think of all the things to do with a beanbag while playing with your toddler.
    - Throw it.
    - Stack it.
    - Put it on your head.
    - Put it on your back.
    - Put it on your stomach.
    - Lie on your back with your feet in the air and balance a beanbag on each foot.
    - Drop it into containers.

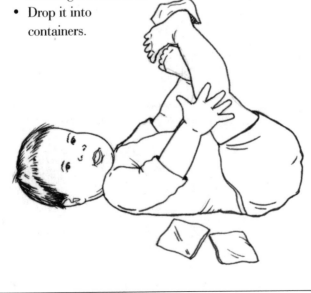

WHAT YOUR TODDLER WILL LEARN:
About Loud and Soft

Creep, Creep, Creep

• Creep on the floor with your toddler. Show him how to creep very softly.

• Place several toys on the floor. Ask your toddler to creep to the toy and wake it up by saying, "Wake up, sleepy head!" and clap his hands.

• Put some stuffed animals on the floor and show him how to creep up to them and pat them on the head to wake them up. Both of you say, "Wake up, sleepy heads!" together.

• Pretend to be one of the animals. Tell your toddler to creep up to you and wake you up.

• This game is lots of fun and your child will want to play it again and again.

Let's Roll!

- Your toddler is in a constant state of motion, crawling, climbing, walking, and running.

- Show your child how to roll. Lie down on the floor and roll from one end to the other. He will be delighted and will want to copy you.

- Play this game. Lie down on the floor side by side. Count to three. On the count of three, say in a big voice, "Let's roll!" Start rolling to the other side of the room.

- It's lots of fun to play, "I'm gonna catch you," by rolling after him across the room.

- Be prepared to play this game often.

- Whenever you do an activity with your toddler, practice it on both right and left sides. Even though toddlers are too young to understand left and right, they can recognize that their bodies have two sides.

WHAT YOUR TODDLER WILL LEARN:
Coordination

The Two-Feet Game

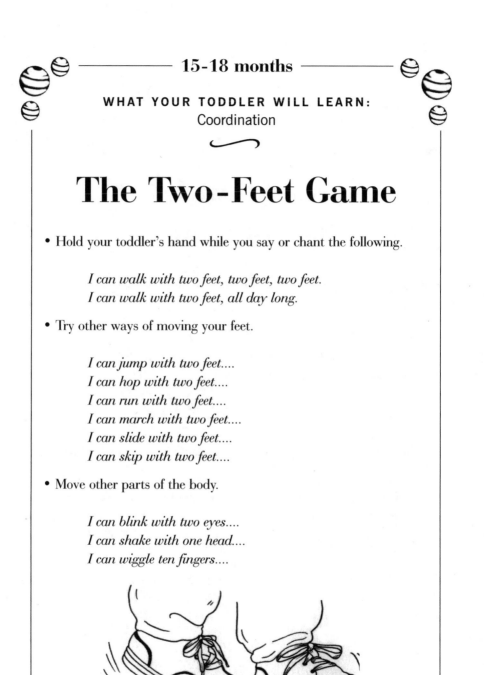

• Hold your toddler's hand while you say or chant the following.

> *I can walk with two feet, two feet, two feet.*
> *I can walk with two feet, all day long.*

• Try other ways of moving your feet.

> *I can jump with two feet....*
> *I can hop with two feet....*
> *I can run with two feet....*
> *I can march with two feet....*
> *I can slide with two feet....*
> *I can skip with two feet....*

• Move other parts of the body.

> *I can blink with two eyes....*
> *I can shake with one head....*
> *I can wiggle ten fingers....*

WHAT YOUR TODDLER WILL LEARN:
Imitation

Finger and Toe Copy Game

- Play this game with your toddler and at least one other person.

- Choose one person to be the leader. Everyone sits opposite the leader, including you with your child on your lap.

- The leader's job is to perform a simple action with his fingers or toes that everyone else can imitate.

- As everyone imitates the leader, encourage your toddler to do so, too.

- Name the person you are imitating: "Daddy is wiggling his finger" or "Susie is wiggling her finger."

- Guide your toddler through the actions until he can perform them alone.

- Using fingers or toes, try wiggling, rolling them in a circular motion, moving them in a grasping motion, shaking or holding them stiff, then relaxing and hitting them together.

WHAT YOUR TODDLER WILL LEARN:
Fine Motor Skills

Paper Rain

- Toddlers love to tear paper. It makes them feel powerful because they can control what is happening to the paper.

- Give your toddler some pages from a used magazine with interesting pictures in it.

- Talk about the pictures and then suggest to your toddler to tear the paper. He may even start tearing before you suggest it.

- When the paper is torn into pieces, pick them up and put them in a container.

- Say to your child, "Here comes the rain." Turn the container over and let the paper "rain" fall out.

- As the rain is falling, sing the song, "Rain, Rain, Go Away."

- Pick up the paper and start again. Your toddler will love this game and want to play it over and over.

Games to Play with Toddlers

Chook, Chook

- This is a wonderful fingerplay that will develop your child's fine motor skills and provide fun for you and your child.

- Sit your toddler on your lap and move his fingers to fit the rhyme.

> *Chook, chook,*
> *Chook, chook, chook,*
> *Good morning, Mrs. Hen,*
> *How many chickens have you got?*
> *Madam, I've got ten.*
> *Four of them are yellow,*
> *And four of them are brown,*
> *And two of them are speckled red*
> *The nicest in the town.*

WHAT YOUR TODDLER WILL LEARN:
Fun

See the Little Spider

- This fingerplay lets you and your toddler share some fun. Walk your fingers along his arms and legs like a crawling spider.

> *See the little spider climbing up the wall.*
>   *(Walk your fingers slowly up your child's arm)*
> *See the little spider stumble and fall.*
>   *(Walk your fingers quickly down your child's arm)*
> *See the little spider tumble down the street.*
>   *(Walk your fingers down your child's leg)*
> *See the little spider stop at your feet.*
>   *(Stop at your child's feet)*

WHAT YOUR TODDLER WILL LEARN:
Thinking Skills

Shoes for Fun

- Take several pairs of shoes that belong to members of your family and put them together in a pile on the floor.

- As you put the shoes down, tell your toddler whose they are.

- He will recognize his own shoes and will probably respond when he sees them.

- Now play the game by asking your child to bring you a particular pair of shoes. "Please bring me daddy's shoes."

- If he doesn't understand, go over to the pile and pick up one of daddy's shoes.

- Not only does this game develop thinking skills, but it also is a hands-on experience in size comparison.

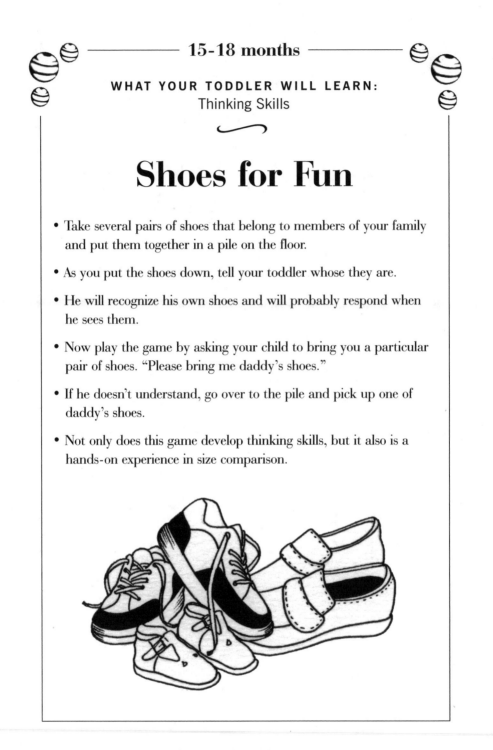

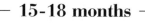

Learning Opposites

- Here are things that you can do to teach your toddler about opposites.
    - Swing him high in the air and say, "High."
    - Swing him low to the ground and say, "Low."
    - Hold your toddler's arms and move them out and say, "Out."
    - Move his arms in and say, "In." Say, "Up" and "Down" as you move his arms and legs up and down.
    - Drop an object in a container and say, "In."
    - Take the object out and say, "Out."

WHAT YOUR TODDLER WILL LEARN:
Problem-Solving Skills

Personal Puzzles

- Give your toddler a large sheet of construction paper or other sturdy paper.

- Give him a crayon and encourage him to draw on the paper.

- Cover his artwork with clear contact paper.

- Cut the paper into two or three pieces, depending on your child's development.

- Give him the puzzle and help him put it together.

- Make puzzles out of sandwiches and slices of cheese.

cover with contact paper and cut into or three pieces.

The Pushing Game

- Find a coffee can with a lid. Cover any sharp edges with duct tape.

- Cut a slot in the lid that is large enough to fit a baby food jar lid.

- Save several baby food jar lids for your toddler to push through the lid of the can.

- Children love to hear the "clank" as the lid hits the bottom of the can.

- Each time you give your child a lid to drop into the can, say, "Here is a circle to drop in the can."

- You could also cover the tops of the baby food lids with red, yellow, and blue construction paper. Each time you give your toddler a lid, say, "Here is a blue circle," or "Here is a red circle."

- If your child is not ready to put the baby food lids through the slot, he will enjoy filling and dumping the coffee can without the lid.

- This is an easy homemade toy that your child will love.

The Tissue Game

- Use a tissue box with about 15 to 20 tissues left.

- Give it to your toddler and let him pull out the tissues. This is great fun for your child.

- Take the tissues that have been pulled from the box and show your child how to roll them into balls.

- Play silly games with the tissue balls. For example, put a ball on your head and let it fall off. Do the same with your toddler.

- Put as many tissue balls as you can in your hand and close it up tight. Say, "Abracadabra" and open your hand so the balls can fall out.

- Be prepared for lots of giggles.

WHAT YOUR TODDLER WILL LEARN:
Fine Motor Skills

Artistry

- Tape a sheet of paper to your toddler's high chair tray (or to a table) and show him how to draw with a crayon.

- Give him a large crayon—the kind that little hands can grasp easily.

- Let him experiment with marking the paper. Each time you give him a crayon, identify its color.

- Play a take-turns game. You make some wavy lines and then your toddler makes his lines.

- As he grows older, he will try to copy your marks.

WHAT YOUR TODDLER WILL LEARN:
Language Skills

Word Book

- Toddlers are developing their vocabularies every day. Sometimes they say words and sometimes they just think them, but they understand many.

- Select several of your toddler's favorite words and find pictures to match them, such as car, doggie, and so on.

- Show the pictures to your child and ask him about them.

- Paste each picture on a separate sheet of paper and make a book for him.

- Your toddler will love looking at the book with you as well as by himself.

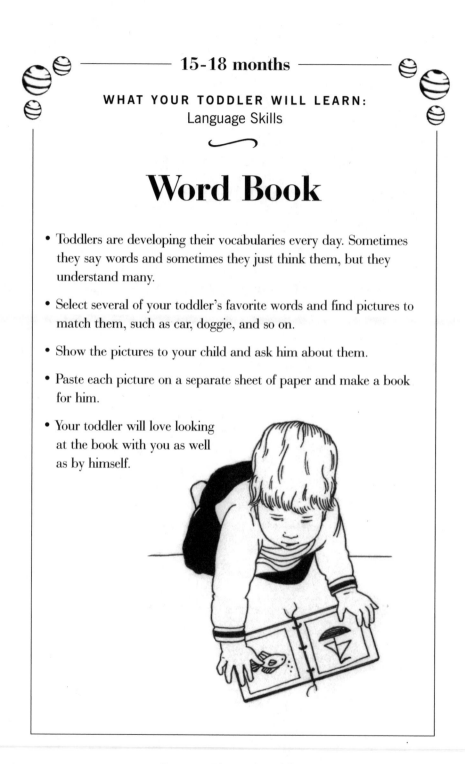

Junk Mail

- Before you throw out that letter enticing you to buy some wonderful food or car or travel experience, save it for your toddler.

- Opening the letter is a challenge and great practice in fine motor skills.

- Unfolding the pieces of literature is exciting. Looking at all of the wonderful pictures and talking about them is a lovely language experience.

- Many toddlers find certain pictures that they love and want to save.

- Make a special mailbox for your toddler's mail.

WHAT YOUR TODDLER WILL LEARN:
Name Recognition

Fill in the Word

- Toddlers at this age can usually say a few words such as "Mama," "Dada," and their own name.

- Make up a story with your child's name in it. Each time you come to his name, ask him to fill in the word.

- For example, "Once upon a time there was a little boy named [your child's name]. This little boy named _____ (let child fill in the word) went to the kitchen to eat his lunch." Keep making up the story and each time say, "This little boy named _____."

- Your child will really love playing this game, as young children love to hear their own names in stories.

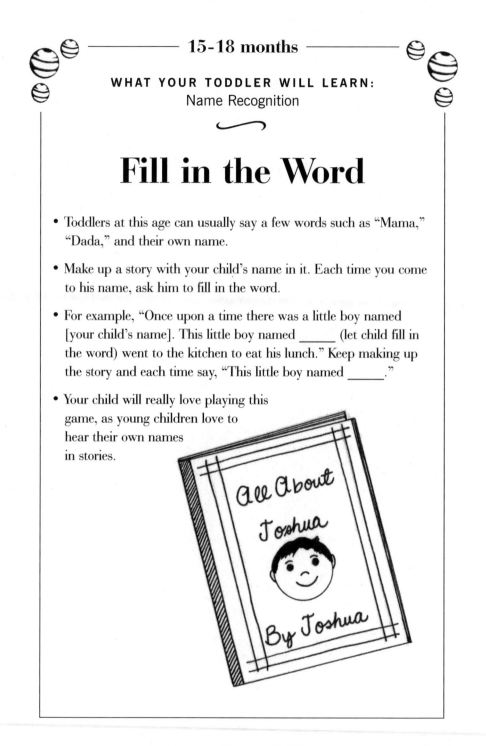

WHAT YOUR TODDLER WILL LEARN:
About Loud and Soft

Megaphone

- This is a great outside game because you can yell.

- Make a megaphone by rolling a large sheet of paper into a cone and taping the ends.

- Sit down with your toddler and speak loudly in the megaphone. "Hello, everybody. How are you?"

- Now give the megaphone to your child and let him speak loudly into the megaphone.

- Hold the megaphone again and repeat the same words, but this time speak very softly.

- Give the megaphone to your child and encourage him to speak softly.

- Say words into the megaphone that your toddler can say. Some of them might be: mama, dada, car, light, bye-bye, and ball.

- Keep saying a word and then giving the megaphone to your child to say a word.

WHAT YOUR TODDLER WILL LEARN:
Language Skills

Car Fun

- Music is fun while riding in the car. Sing favorite songs or listen to your toddler's most loved tapes.

- If your child knows a nursery rhyme or song well, sing it and leave out a word. For example, "Mary had a little _____." Or "Twinkle, twinkle, little _____."

- Once your toddler can fill in the missing word, show him how to change its sound by singing loudly or softly.

- Try singing a familiar song and leave out a word in the middle of a sentence instead of at the end.

Looking Out the Window

- This game helps toddlers look for specific things while riding in a car. Recite this rhyme.

   I'm looking out the window,
   I'm looking out the window,
   I'm looking out the window,
   And this is what I see.

- After you say, "And this is what I see," say, "I see a car." Then ask your toddler, "Do you see the car?"

- The purpose of this game is to direct your toddler's attention to things that he can see outside the car. Repeat the rhyme and direct your toddler's attention to other objects such as the street, people, animals, colors, and so on.

Peekaboo Car

- Peekaboo is a great game that children seem to enjoy until about age three.

- This version is ideal for the car and will keep your toddler occupied as well as sharpen his visual skills.

- Play peekaboo with parts of the car. Tell your toddler to cover his eyes and play peekaboo with the window.

- Suggest different parts of the car, such as the wipers, the radio, the seatbelt, and so on. Then explore what you see out the window. Say, "Play peekaboo with that lady," or "Play peekaboo with the bridge."

- Ask your toddler, "Where is the sun? Can you play peekaboo with the sun?"

Finger Talk

- This game keeps your child occupied in the car or while waiting at the doctor's office, and it develops his language.

- Draw a face on each of your child's thumbs with a non-toxic marker.

- Name the thumb puppets so that you can talk to them. "Hello, funny face," or "How are you, Billy?"

- Talk to the thumb puppets. Your toddler can talk back or just move his thumbs up and down in reply.

- The following are a few things to say to the puppets.
    - Do you see that red car?
    - Look at the beautiful trees.
    - Red light, stop; green light, go.

- Ask the puppets to sing songs with you.

- You can also draw faces on your fingers and wiggle them back and forth like puppets talking.

- Changing the tone and tempo of your voice will delight your child.

- The finger puppets can give directions, ask questions, or sing songs.

WHAT YOUR TODDLER WILL LEARN
Fine Motor Skills

Pop-Up Toy

- Make a pop-up toy for your toddler. Make a hole in the bottom of a paper cup. Put a straw through the hole.

- Attach a round piece of cardboard to one end of the straw. Draw a face on the cardboard.

- Show your toddler how to pull the straw and make the face disappear and push up on the straw and make the face appear.

② Attach a round piece of cardboard and draw a face on it.

① Cut a hole in the bottom of the paper cup.

③ push straw up and down to make the face appear and dissapear.

Looking Through the Window

- Cut two holes into one side of a cardboard box such as a shoebox.

- On the opposite side, cut a "window."

- Show your toddler how to look through the paired holes.

- While he looks through the holes, look through the "window." What fun to see a familiar face!

- Stick your finger through the window and wiggle it as he watches.

- He will soon learn to watch through the paired holes while putting things through the window from the other side.

Choo, Choo

- Spread a large beach towel on the floor.

- Sit your toddler on the towel. Use the towel to pull him very slowly across the floor.

- Pretend with him that he is traveling in something. If it's a car, make a car sound. If it's an airplane, make an airplane sound. If it's a train, make a "choo, choo" sound.

- Even though toddlers may not understand the mode of transportation, they enjoy making the sounds.

"Choo, Choo!"

A Remarkable Discovery

- Toddlers enjoy learning how to identify the different parts of their bodies. The most remarkable part of this discovery is that they learn that they are a person just like you.

- Stand in front of a mirror with your child.

- Point to his nose and say, "Here is [child's name's] nose. Now point to your nose and say, "Here is daddy's nose."

- Turn your child around so he is facing you and ask him to touch your nose.

- When he touches your nose, say, "Your nose is just like daddy's nose."

- Continue the game with a different part of the body.

WHAT YOUR TODDLER WILL LEARN:
About Sharing

Sharing Game

- Sit on the floor opposite your child.

- Give the child an object such as a favorite toy and say, "This is for you."

- After your child has had a chance to explore it, say, "Will you please give it back to me?"

- The child will give you the toy.

- Repeat the game.

Games to Play with Toddlers

WHAT YOUR TODDLER WILL LEARN:
About Object Permanence

Where's the Bunny?

- Hide a favorite toy (any stuffed animal) while your toddler watches.

- Ask the child, "Where's the bunny?" Encourage him to find the toy and give it to you.

- Move the bunny to a different place as he watches. Ask him again to find the toy.

- Ask the child, "Where shall we put the bunny next?"

- As you play this game, your child will begin to copy the hiding places that you have established as well as find some new ones.

- Increase the challenge by adding more objects. For example, put the bunny, a hat, and a block around the room and tell your toddler to find the hat.

- Ask your child to bring other objects from around the room.

WHAT YOUR TODDLER WILL LEARN:
Thinking Skills

Where Is the Toy?

• Put two dishtowels in front of your toddler.

• Put one of his favorite toys, such as a ball, under one of the towels.

• Ask your child, "Where is the ball?" Lift up the towel that has the ball under it.

• Repeat this several times and you will soon find that your child will be lifting the towel before you have a chance.

• Add a third towel to make the game a little harder.

Games to Play with Toddlers

WHAT YOUR TODDLER WILL LEARN:
About Spatial Concepts

Animals All Around

- Sit on the floor next to your toddler.

- Put a box in front of the two of you.

- Take a stuffed animal and put it next to the box. As you do this, tell your child that you are putting the toy next to the box.

- Now, ask your toddler to give you the toy that is next to the box.

- Continue putting the stuffed animal in different places—in front of the box, behind the box, on top of the box, and under the box.

- Next, give the toy to your child and ask him to put the toy in different places around the box.

- When your child does this easily, add more boxes so that the game will become more challenging.

WHAT YOUR TODDLER WILL LEARN:
About Empty and Full

Toy Transfer Game

- Place two large containers on opposite sides of a room.

- Fill one container with small toys.

- Have a third container that is easy to carry, such as a basket with a handle.

- Show your toddler how to load the toys from the full container into the basket, carry them across the room, and dump them into the empty container.

- He may have to make more than one trip to empty the toy basket. When it is empty, say, "All gone!"

- Repeat the activity. Say, "All gone!" whenever he empties a basket.

- As you repeat this game a few times, try using the words "empty" and "full."

WHAT YOUR TODDLER WILL LEARN:
Listening Skills

Doll Play

- Following directions is difficult for toddlers because it requires listening and doing something at the same time. Doll play is a good way to practice this skill.

- Give your toddler his favorite doll or stuffed animal and ask him to identify the parts of its body: "Where is the doll's head, ears, legs, tummy," and so on.

- Suggest he do specific things with the doll.
    - Brush the doll's hair.
    - Tickle the doll's tummy.
    - Wash the doll's face.
    - Brush the doll's teeth.

- Not only will your toddler improve his listening skills, but he also will practice the nurturing behavior that he has experienced as your child.

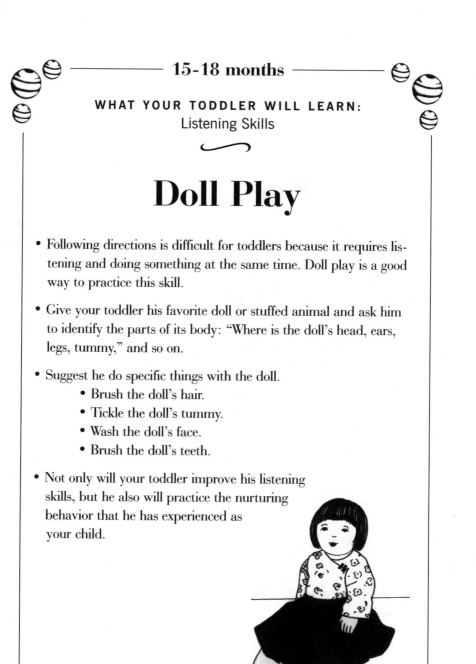

Purse Toys

- Some of the best toys can be found right in your own home.

- Toddlers love to explore purses.

- Fill an empty purse with familiar things, such as keys, comb, tissue, eyeglasses (remove the lenses), and money purse.

- Ask your child to find an item in the purse. For example, "Would you please give me the car keys?"

- When your child finds the keys, praise him for finding them.

Teddy Swing

- Tie a length of string or ribbon under the arms of a teddy bear or favorite stuffed animal.

- Tie the other end of the string or ribbon to a tree limb to suspend the bear about two feet off the ground.

- Show your toddler how to push the teddy gently to make it swing.

- While enjoying this game very much, children also begin to understand that their push causes the teddy to move.

Mine and Yours

- It's been said that a toddler's philosophy of life is "What's mine is mine, what's yours is mine, what's his is mine."

- Learning the difference between "mine" and "yours" will come more easily if you help your child know which objects are definitely his and which objects are yours.

- Gather together objects that belong to you, such as your purse, your comb, and your glasses. Mix them up with several of your child's belongings.

- Ask your child, "Will you please give me my glasses?" When he gives them to you, say, "Thank you. These are my glasses. They are mine."

- Now give your child one of his toys and say, "This is your doll. It is yours."

- Continue with the rest of the objects.

- This game is a gentle way of teaching "yours" and "mine."

WHAT YOUR TODDLER WILL LEARN:
Language Skills

Hello! Who's There?

- Find a toy telephone that your child can play with on his own or with you.

- Say, "Ding-a-ling, ding-a-ling." Pretend the phone is ringing and answer it.

- As you are talking to the imaginary person (someone the baby knows, such as grandparents or a friend), also talk to your child. For example, say, "Hello, Grandpa," then say to your child, "It's your grandpa." Talk about a special activity, a visit, a meal, or maybe plans for the day. Be sure your toddler understands the topic.

- Be sure to say, "Good-bye," and hang up the phone.

- Give the phone to your child and encourage him to have an imaginary conversation.

WHAT YOUR TODDLER WILL LEARN:
Language Skills

"Go Truck"

- A toddler is beginning to express language. Words and short sentences make an exciting new development in his thinking. He is learning to connect nouns and verbs such as, "read book," "bounce ball," and "go truck."

- Sit on the floor with your toddler and put a favorite toy in front of you. Think of action words to go with the toy and perform the action.

- For example, start with a car or truck. Say "Go truck" and move the truck. You could also say:
    - "Turn truck" and turn the truck.
    - "Fall truck" and gently knock the truck down (this always gets a laugh).
    - "Go slowly truck" and move the truck slowly.

- You can play this game with a stuffed toy, blocks, and many other toys.

WHAT YOUR TODDLER WILL LEARN:
Language Skills

Puppet Fun

- With a small hand puppet, you can play many games with your toddler. After you have played, you will find your child playing the games by himself.

- Fit the puppet on your hand and talk to your toddler in a disguised voice. Ask him questions about himself, such as "What's your name?" or "Can you wave bye-bye?"

- Give the puppet to your toddler and suggest ways to play with it. "Can you make the puppet lie down?" "Can you make the puppet go to sleep?" "Can you make the puppet jump up and down?"

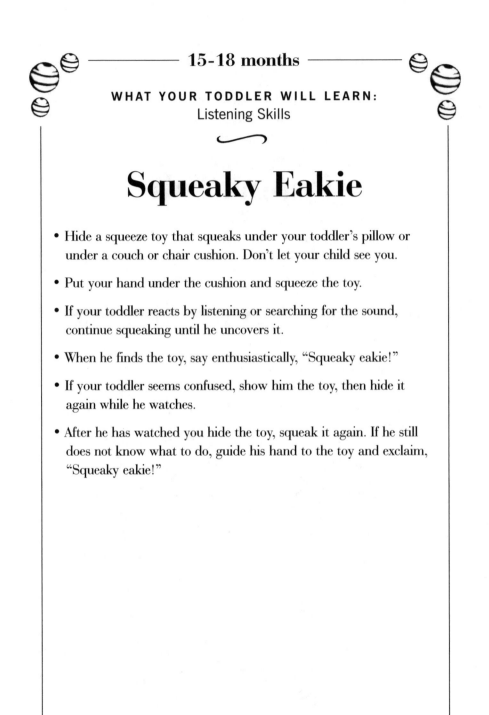

WHAT YOUR TODDLER WILL LEARN:
Listening Skills

Squeaky Eakie

- Hide a squeeze toy that squeaks under your toddler's pillow or under a couch or chair cushion. Don't let your child see you.

- Put your hand under the cushion and squeeze the toy.

- If your toddler reacts by listening or searching for the sound, continue squeaking until he uncovers it.

- When he finds the toy, say enthusiastically, "Squeaky eakie!"

- If your toddler seems confused, show him the toy, then hide it again while he watches.

- After he has watched you hide the toy, squeak it again. If he still does not know what to do, guide his hand to the toy and exclaim, "Squeaky eakie!"

WHAT YOUR TODDLER WILL LEARN:
Coordination

Teddy Bear Sandwiches

- Invite your toddler and teddy to lunch.

- With your toddler's help, cut heart shapes out of whole wheat bread with a valentine-shaped cookie cutter.

- Cut off the point of the heart, and the bread will look like a teddy bear face.

- Spread the teddy bear with peanut butter.

- Make a face with raisins and other nutritious foods.

Cut heart shapes out of whole wheat bread, then cut off the "point" of the heart.

Spread with peanut butter and make a face with nutritious foods.

The Muffin Man

- The song "Do You Know the Muffin Man" is extremely popular with toddlers. They like to sing it and dance to it.

- Put some mini muffins in a basket on the table.

- Sing the words:

  Do you know the muffin man, the muffin man, the muffin man?
  Do you know the muffin man who lives in Drury Lane?

- Take your child's hand as you sing and go to the muffin basket.

- Then sing:

  Yes, I know the muffin man, the muffin man, the muffin man.
  Oh, yes I know the muffin man who lives in Drury lane.

- Share a muffin with your child.

WHAT YOUR TODDLER WILL LEARN:
Observation Skills

Look Closely

- Sit at a table with your toddler and tell him that you want to do something special.

- Hold an orange in your hand and talk about its name and color.

- Give the orange to your child. Ask him to smell the orange and feel it with his hand. Talk about the smell and feel.

- Peel and open the orange. Show the sections to your child. Give him a section and show him its membrane and seeds.

- Eat a section and ask your child if he would like a taste, too.

Games to Play with Toddlers

WHAT YOUR TODDLER WILL LEARN:
To Use a Spoon

Spoon Feeding

- Eating with a spoon is an important social skill for your toddler.

- Before you attempt to teach your child how to use a spoon, give him spoons to play with.

- He will bang them, drop them, and probably put them in his mouth.

- When you think he is ready to play this game, put a small piece of banana on a spoon and put it in your mouth.

- Put a small piece of banana on a spoon and put it in your child's mouth.

- Put a spoon in his hand with a small piece of banana on it. Guide the spoon to his mouth.

- Keep playing this game with different kinds of food and soon your child will be putting the spoon in a bowl of food and feeding himself.

WHAT YOUR TODDLER WILL LEARN:
Coordination

Watch the Rain

- Give a small cup full of water to your toddler while he sits in the bathtub.

- Hold a slotted spoon or colander in front of him, and ask him to pour the water into it.

- Next, let him hold the spoon or colander while you pour the "rain" over it.

- Continue playing the game, taking turns pouring the water through the spoon or colander.

Games to Play with Toddlers

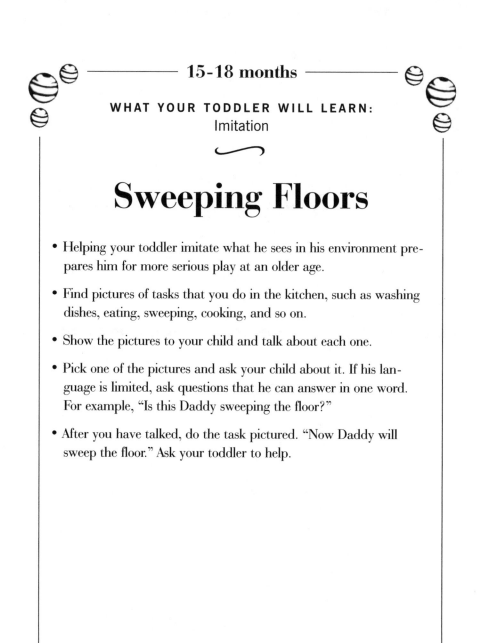

WHAT YOUR TODDLER WILL LEARN:
Imitation

Sweeping Floors

- Helping your toddler imitate what he sees in his environment prepares him for more serious play at an older age.

- Find pictures of tasks that you do in the kitchen, such as washing dishes, eating, sweeping, cooking, and so on.

- Show the pictures to your child and talk about each one.

- Pick one of the pictures and ask your child about it. If his language is limited, ask questions that he can answer in one word. For example, "Is this Daddy sweeping the floor?"

- After you have talked, do the task pictured. "Now Daddy will sweep the floor." Ask your toddler to help.

WHAT YOUR TODDLER WILL LEARN:
Bonding

Good Night, Sleep Tight

- This is a nice rhyme to say to your toddler before you put him to bed.

- It's a good idea to say the same rhyme each night. Toddlers love consistency.

> *Good night, sleep tight,*
> *Don't let the bedbugs bite.*
> *If they bite,*
> *Squeeze them tight.*
> *Good night, sleep tight.*

WHAT YOUR TODDLER WILL LEARN:
Creativity

Make-Believe House

- Make a tent or a playhouse for your child. Drape a sheet over a card table or the backs of two or more chairs to make a simple tent.

- If you want more detail, make walls and a roof out of felt for the card table. Decorate the walls.

- Pretend that the tent is a cave, an airplane, a train, a spaceship, or a house.

- Take a pillow, blanket, and stuffed toy inside your make-believe house.

WHAT YOUR TODDLER WILL LEARN:
Nature Appreciation

Outside Treasures

- There are so many treasures outdoors. Take a basket and go exploring with your toddler.

- As you find things, put them into the treasure basket. Stones, seedpods, twigs, leaves, flowers, pebbles, and shells are just a few of the many treasures you will discover.

- After you have gathered several treasures, take each one out and talk about it.

- Pay close attention to the treasures that your toddler seems particularly interested in, to give you ideas for future learning experiences.

- Ask your toddler for one of the treasures to return to the basket. See if he can remember its name.

WHAT YOUR TODDLER WILL LEARN:
Fun

Blowing Bubbles

- An inexpensive jar of bubble liquid will provide hours of giggles for you and your toddler. Try the following:
    - Blow bubbles outside on both a calm day and a windy day.
    - Make bubbles by waving the bubble wand in the air rather than blowing through it.
    - See how many bubbles you can catch on the wand.
    - See how many bubbles you can count at one time.
    - Blow bubbles in front of a fan.
    - Try to catch all the bubbles before they reach the ground.
    - Step on the bubbles. Where do they go when they pop?

- Teach your toddler to blow bubbles. Practice in shaping his mouth to blow will promote language development.

WHAT YOUR TODDLER WILL LEARN:
Nature Appreciation

The Dandelion Game

- Take your child on a dandelion walk.

- Pick a dandelion to hold. See how many more dandelions you can find along your walk.

- Examine the dandelion with your child. Look at it through a magnifying glass.

- Use words such as "delicately" and "gently" to describe how to hold a dandelion.

- Pick a bouquet of dandelions to put in a vase at home.

- Compare the dandelions to other yellow things in your house.

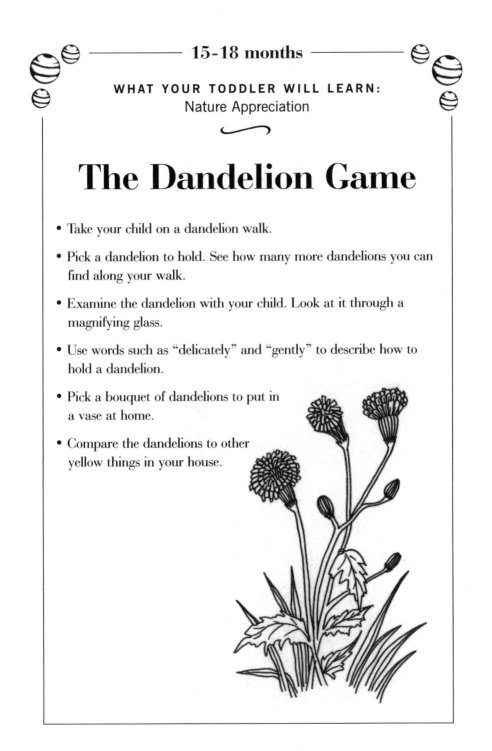

WHAT YOUR TODDLER WILL LEARN:
Eye-Hand Coordination

Sprinkle Time

• Poke holes into the bottom of a large plastic bottle.

• Go outside with your toddler and talk about the grass, the flowers, and all the things in your yard.

• Fill the plastic bottle with water from the hose and tell your child where to sprinkle the water.

• Ask your child to sprinkle the grass, the sidewalk, the flowers, and so on. Each time your toddler understands your directions, praise him.

WHAT YOUR TODDLER WILL LEARN:
Responsibility

Get the Beanbag

- This game can be played with one or more people. You will need a basket and some beanbags.

- Your task is to toss the beanbags into the basket. Your toddler's task is to take the beanbags out of the basket and give them back to you.

- If your toddler is walking, he will more easily remove the beanbags without your help.

- If your toddler is not yet walking, tip the basket to help him remove the beanbags.

- Soon your little cherub will be trying to throw the beanbags himself.

WHAT YOUR TODDLER WILL LEARN:
Bonding

Baby Bird

• This is a nice game to play outside in warm weather.

• Sit down on the grass with your toddler curled up in your lap.

• You pretend to be the big bird and your toddler is the baby bird.

• Pretend to be asleep and then wake up. Say to your child, "Come on, baby bird, it's time to fly." Very slowly get up and flap your arms like wings. Fly around the yard and then say to your toddler, "Let's fly to the tree." Give specific directions to help your toddler learn the names of objects in the yard.

• Whisper to your baby bird, "It's time to go back to the nest."

• Go back to where you were sitting, and let your baby bird curl back into your arms.

• Repeat this game over and over. You might even ask your baby bird to fly by himself, then come back to the nest.

WHAT YOUR TODDLER WILL LEARN:
Coordination

The Line Game

- Lines can be made in sand, dirt, and mud.

- Show your toddler how to make a line in the dirt with his finger.

- Guide his hand gently to help him make a line.

- Next, make a wiggly line. Help your toddler do the same.

- Try making lines with other objects such as a stick or a toy.

- Push a toy car through the dirt and show your toddler the tire tracks.

- These experiences acquaint your child with lines and develop eye-hand coordination.

18-21 months

Fit the Pieces

- This is a game that your toddler will enjoy playing over and over.

- Collect several cookie cutters. Try to get shapes that your toddler will recognize, such as animals or holiday figures and objects.

- Start by tracing around one cookie cutter with a marker. Give your toddler the cookie cutter that matches the shape you drew. Show her how they fit together.

- After tracing several cookie cutters and showing how they match, give your toddler two cookie cutters and one tracing and see whether she can choose the matching cookie cutter.

- Once she understands, add another tracing and another cookie cutter.

Games to Play with Toddlers

WHAT YOUR TODDLER WILL LEARN:
To Put Puzzles Together

Puzzle Pieces

- Collect cardboard party decorations such as Halloween characters, birthday scenes, and Valentines.

- Cut each decoration in two, like pieces of a puzzle.

- Cut so that the pieces are all different shapes.

- Give your toddler one piece. Mix up the others and spread them on the floor.

- Talk with your toddler about the piece in her hand—its color, shape, and other features.

- Help her find the matching piece. Continue playing the game with another piece. Keep helping her until she plays by herself.

Car Pockets

- Sew several pockets on a pillowcase using scraps of material or felt.

- From additional felt, cut out shapes and figures of animals and people small enough to fit into the pockets. Decorate the cutouts.

- Give your toddler the pillowcase while riding in the car. She will enjoy playing with the animals and people.

- Before you start driving, show your child how to hide the felt pieces in the pockets, and how to peek their heads out.

- If you reserve this game only for the car, it will be a special game.

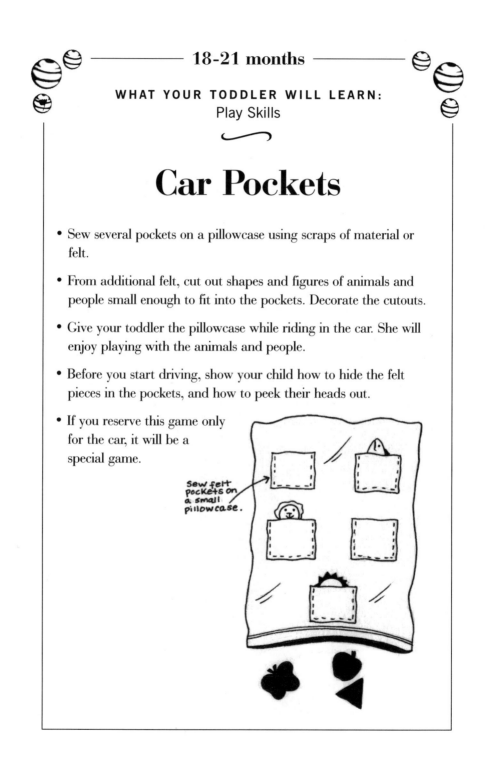

Sew felt pockets on a small pillowcase.

WHAT YOUR TODDLER WILL LEARN:
Fine Motor Skills

The Raisin Game

- Raisins are a nutritious food and they make great objects for fine motor skill development.

- Fill a small plastic bowl with raisins.

- Next to the bowl place a plastic jar with a lid. Be sure that the lid is loose so that your child will be able to remove it easily.

- Ask your toddler to put a raisin in the jar. In order for her to do this, she will have to remove the lid.

- After she has transferred all of the raisins to the jar, she can dump them out and start again.

- A young child can work at this activity for a long time.

Unwrapping Game

- Wrap a ball or a toy in colorful paper.

- Show the wrapped toy to your toddler and ask, "What do you think is inside?"

- Give the wrapped toy to your child to remove the paper.

- This is difficult for a young child, and she will be enthralled by the effort. The sound of the paper might interest her more than the toy itself.

- Gather several kinds of paper such as tissue, foil, wrapping paper, and newspaper.

- Take the toy that your child unwrapped and wrap it in another kind of paper while she watches.

- Let her unwrap again. Continue until she tires of the game.

Matching Game

- Give your toddler three identical objects, such as teaspoons.

- Pick up each spoon, name it, and pretend that you are eating something.

- Let your child hold each spoon, feeling its shape and texture.

- Replace one spoon with a fork. Ask her to give you the spoon. Ask for another spoon.

- Pick up the fork and say its name. Pretend to eat with it. Let your child hold the fork and feel its shape and texture.

- Put out two spoons and a fork. Ask your child to give you the fork. Praise her when she selects the correct one.

WHAT YOUR TODDLER WILL LEARN:
Coordination

Tongs Game

- Gather a group of small toys into a large box or bowl.

- Give your toddler a pair of kitchen tongs and show her how to pick up the objects with the tongs.

- Once your child easily picks up a toy with the tongs, show her how to move the toy into a different box.

- Place a muffin tin next to the box. Show her how to put a toy into a muffin cup using the tongs. This takes a great deal of coordination.

- This type of game also helps develop counting skills.

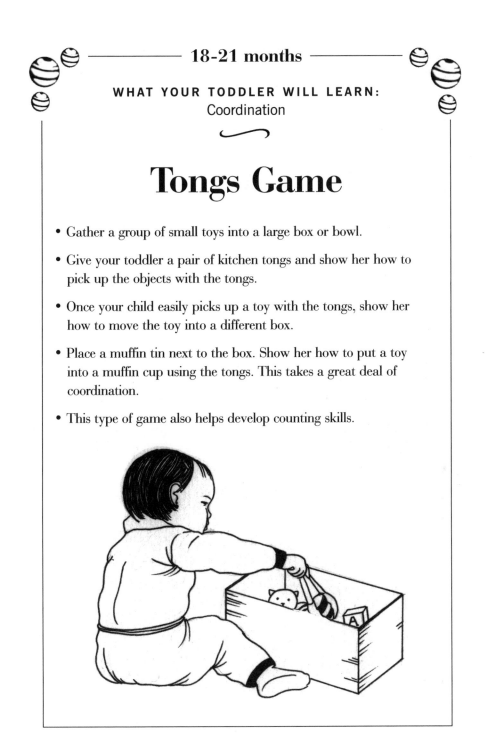

Games to Play with Toddlers

WHAT YOUR TODDLER WILL LEARN:
Listening Skills

The Radio Game

- What does a toddler love to do? You're right. Turn dials and push buttons.

- Turning a radio dial can be a source of fun and enjoyment. It also helps develop your child's listening skills.

- Show your child how to turn the dial to get different kinds of music.

- Play a game. Your toddler turns the dial or pushes the button until you say, "Stop."

- When you stop, dance according to the kind of music that is playing.

WHAT YOUR TODDLER WILL LEARN:
Spatial Awareness

Understanding Places

- If you tell your toddler that an object is on the table, it is not the same as having your child take the object and put it on the table.

- If your little one carries objects from one place to another and then back again, she will begin to learn where a place is.

- Give your child a small basket and ask her to place it on the table.

- Ask your child to bring the basket to you. When she brings it to you, put something colorful in the basket. An interesting scarf or lightweight colorful block will do just fine.

- Now ask her to return the basket to the table.

- Keep playing the game and each time she brings you the basket, put something different in the basket.

Clapping Games

- There are many ways to clap with your child. Pick a song that is fun to sing, such as "This Old Man," and experiment with all the different ways that you can clap.

- Put your toddler in your lap with her palms down on your palms. As you sing the song, clap your hands upward to hers.

- Put your hands in front of your toddler and clap them together.

- Take your toddler's hands and let them clap on yours.

- Take your toddler's hands and clap them together.

WHAT YOUR TODDLER WILL LEARN:
Rhythm

Moving to Music

- Talking, reading, and moving all improve when children learn and practice rhythm activities.

- Play some instrumental music and move with your child. If the music is fast, move quickly. If the music is slow, move slowly.

- Encourage her to copy your actions. Say, "Can you turn like me?" or "Can you bend like me?"

- Vary the musical sounds from high to low, loud to soft, and fast to slow.

Listen to the Sound

- There are many sounds inside and outside. It is important to help a toddler begin to differentiate the sounds.

- Take a sound walk through your house and point out the different sounds to your child.

- You will be amazed at all the sounds in your home.

- Here are some sounds that you might hear.

• Radio playing	• Lights buzzing
• Dishwasher running	• Clock ticking
• Rain falling	• Dog barking
• Refrigerator running	• Furnace running
• Doorbell ringing	• Telephone ringing
• Sirens blaring	• Birds singing
• Computer humming	• Person coughing
• Toilet flushing	

Whispering

- Toddlers are fascinated by whispering. They are very proud of themselves when they can do it.

- Whispering helps children learn to modulate their voice. It takes a lot of concentration.

- Whisper something to your toddler. Say, "Let's read a book."

- Ask your toddler to whisper something back to you.

- Keep whispering to each other until your toddler understands how to make her voice very soft.

WHAT YOUR TODDLER WILL LEARN:
Language Skills

Paint the World

• Give your toddler a paintbrush and pail of water outside.

• Let your child paint the house with water.

• Paint the sidewalk, porch, mailbox, car, and whatever else can be "painted" with water.

Paint With Your Feet

• Spread a large sheet of paper outside.

• Set big sponges in a large, shallow tray next to the paper. Pour tempera paint onto the sponges.

• No brushes, just feet! Hold your child's hand and show her how to dip one foot into the paint. Hold your toddler's hand as she walks across the paper in case it's a little slippery.

• Try this with several different colors of paint, or put paint on a ball and roll it across the paper, or make hand prints.

WHAT YOUR TODDLER WILL LEARN:
Imagination

Art Outdoors

- Take a baking pan filled with sand or salt outside.

- Encourage your toddler to draw in the pan with her fingers. When she tires of her drawings, shake the pan to erase them.

- On another day, bring an easel, paint, paper, and brushes outdoors. Encourage your child to experiment with painting on the easel. When her painting is finished, hang it up to dry.

Color Stickies

- Get a roll of double-sided tape, the kind that is sticky on both sides.

- Make two balls out of the tape for you and your toddler. Give one of the balls to your child.

- Show her how it sticks to things by putting it on different parts of your body.

- Take two pieces of construction paper and put them in front of your child. The papers should be contrasting colors.

- Stick your ball on the red paper and say, "The ball is on the red paper. Can you stick your ball on the red paper?"

- Repeat with the second color.

WHAT YOUR TODDLER WILL LEARN:
About Colors

Colors and Shapes

- Cut out several circles from red and yellow construction paper.

- Put the red circles on the floor in front of your toddler.

- Put your hands on the circles. Touch them one at a time.

- Say, "I am putting my hands on the red circle."

- Add the yellow circles.

- Put your feet on the yellow circles and say, "I am putting my feet on the yellow circles."

- With your toddler, play this game of touching the red circles with your hands and the yellow circles with your feet.

Magic Mud

- In a dishpan or unbreakable bowl, mix a box of cornstarch with enough water to achieve the consistency of bread dough.

- Say to your toddler, "Let's be very quiet and watch some magic."

- If you roll the mixture, it forms a ball. If you let it rest, it dissolves to liquid.

- Enjoy exploring the properties of Magic Mud.

WHAT YOUR TODDLER WILL LEARN:
Creativity

Playdough Experiments

- The kitchen is a great place to experiment with playdough.

- Show your child how to roll a piece of playdough and squeeze it, pound it, poke it, and pull it apart.

- Give your child some tools to use with the playdough, such as a Popsicle stick for poking, cutting, scraping, and scooping. She can use a rolling pin with both hands to flatten the dough.

- With cookie cutters, your child can make "pretend cookies" for teddy bears.

Fun with Streamers

- Crepe paper streamers are wonderful toys for toddlers. Here are some ways to play with them outside.

- Put masking tape around the end of the streamer to create a "handle" so the dye from the streamer does not get on the toddler's hands.
    - Run with a streamer in your hand.
    - Twirl a streamer around in your hand.
    - Hold the streamer low to the ground and encourage your child to jump over it.
    - Tie several streamers to a tree branch low enough so that your child can jump up and hit them.
    - On a windy day, simply hold the streamer in the air and watch it ripple in the wind.

Blowing Games

- Toddlers enjoy blowing. While it requires skill to learn, practice also strengthens the mouth for language development. The following are some ways for your child to blow.
  - Blow air through straws.
  - Blow bubbles in a large cup of water.
  - Blow on your fingers.
  - Blow on one finger.
  - Blow air into a paper sack.
  - Blow a leaf off your hand.
  - Blow a small, lightweight ball around the room with a straw.
  - Blow a flower or blade of grass.

The Catalog Game

• Select a catalog with a variety of pictures of things with which your child is familiar.

• Take turns picking something for the other person to be, for example, a dog.

• If you choose a picture of a dog, then your toddler has to pretend to be a dog.

• Another idea is to tape pictures on 3 x 5 index cards and turn this into a card game.

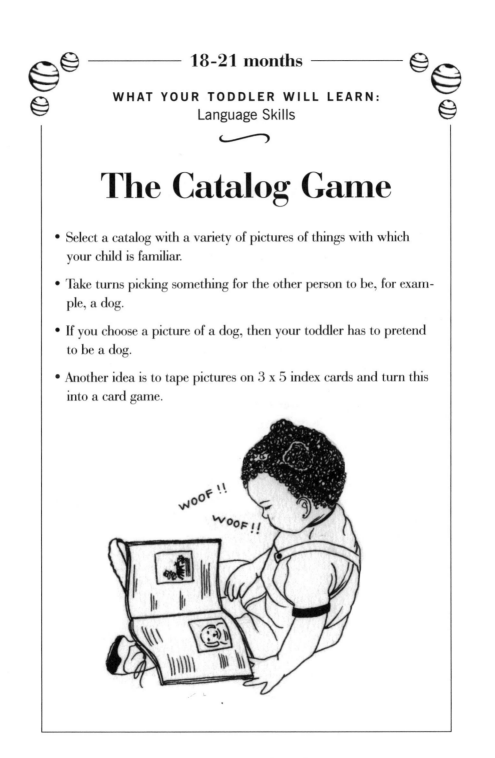

Games to Play with Toddlers

Hard and Soft

- Tactile stimulation is a very important part of a child's development. By understanding how things feel, young children develop language and cognitive thinking.

- Toddlers can begin to understand if something is hard or soft.

- Give your toddler soft objects one at a time. Each time you give her an object, say the word "soft" in a gentle voice.

- Start with cotton balls, stuffed animals, or pieces of soft material.

- Now give your toddler things to feel that are hard. Each time you give her the object, say the word "hard" in a different voice than the soft voice.

- A hard, small toy or block is good to use.

- After you have played this game a few times, put a soft and a hard object in a paper sack. Let your child take one of the objects out of the sack and see if she can tell you if it is hard or soft.

Body Stickers

- This game will help your child become aware of her body.

- Present your toddler with a variety of sticky things—Band-Aids, stickers, tape, labels, and other sticky objects, and stickers with happy faces or animals that your child recognizes.

- Give one to your child and show her how to stick it onto her body.

- Tell her to place the sticker on her tummy and encourage her to push her tummy in and out.

- Tell her to place the sticker on her cheek and puff in and out.

- Other places to put stickers:
    - Toes—and wiggle them.
    - Elbows—and move them up and down.
    - Palms—and open and close them.

Do What I Do

- Play a game of imitation with your toddler.

- Perform different actions and encourage your child to imitate you. For example, wave your hands, wiggle your fingers, stomp your feet, and pretend to be asleep.

- Encourage your toddler do something while you imitate her. At first, you may have to make suggestions. Suggest easy movements such as waving bye-bye or clapping hands.

- Adapt this activity to jobs such as raking leaves, dusting, and sweeping.

WHAT YOUR TODDLER WILL LEARN:
Listening Skills

Stuffed Fun

- Ask your toddler to get her favorite stuffed animal and put it on the floor next to her.

- Sit down on the floor and place a stuffed toy in front of yourself.

- Ask your child to do different activities with her stuffed toy. If your toddler doesn't understand, show her by following the direction yourself.

- Here are some ideas: pick up your animal's arm, shake its leg, nod its head, move its knee, move its elbow, and give it a big hug.

Games to Play with Toddlers

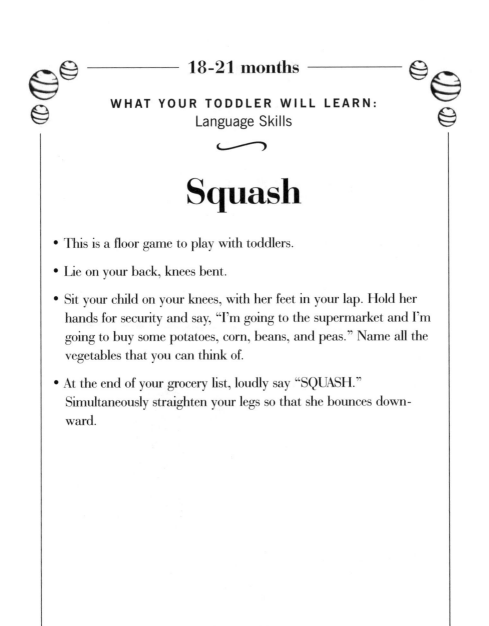

WHAT YOUR TODDLER WILL LEARN:
Language Skills

Squash

- This is a floor game to play with toddlers.

- Lie on your back, knees bent.

- Sit your child on your knees, with her feet in your lap. Hold her hands for security and say, "I'm going to the supermarket and I'm going to buy some potatoes, corn, beans, and peas." Name all the vegetables that you can think of.

- At the end of your grocery list, loudly say "SQUASH." Simultaneously straighten your legs so that she bounces downward.

WHAT YOUR TODDLER WILL LEARN:
Body Awareness

The Jungle Game

- Get down on the floor with your toddler and demonstrate how to squirm like a snake.

- Set a chair in the middle of the floor and slither around it with your toddler.

- Try making a tunnel to slither through by placing two or three chairs side by side and covering them with a blanket.

- Squirm through the tunnel with your toddler.

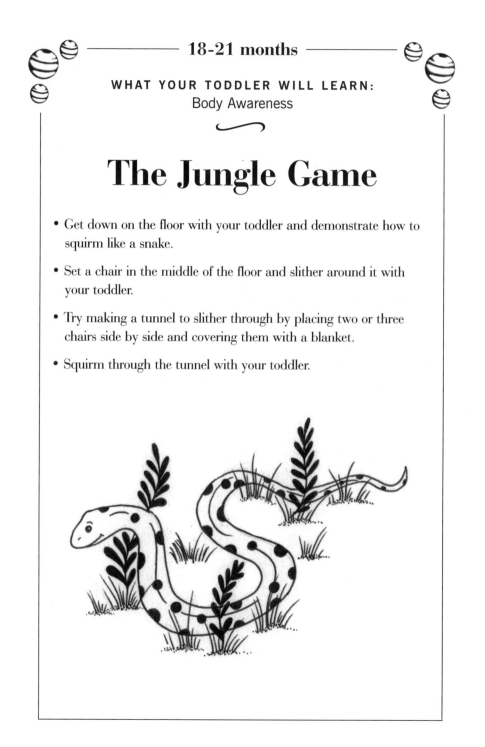

Games to Play with Toddlers

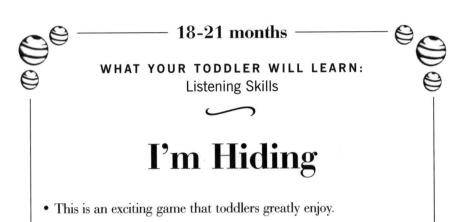

WHAT YOUR TODDLER WILL LEARN:
Listening Skills

I'm Hiding

- This is an exciting game that toddlers greatly enjoy.

- At a moment when your toddler is not looking, hide close by and say, "I'm hiding, come and find me."

- Hide behind something that leaves you partially visible, such as a bush, a tree, or the side of a house.

- Your child will learn to listen for the direction of your voice, then use her eyes to find you.

- This game also helps your toddler understand that a visible shoulder and arm are attached to a whole body.

- Your toddler will be so thrilled to find you. It's a perfect time for a big hug.

Cat and Mouse

- Tell your toddler that you are a tiny little mouse and that she is the cat that is going to chase you.

- Tell your toddler that the mouse says, "Squeak, squeak" and the cat says, "Meow, meow."

- Get down on the floor and say, "You can't catch me!" Start crawling fast and encourage your child to chase you.

- Crawl behind furniture, under tables, and into other rooms.

- When your child understands the game, switch parts.

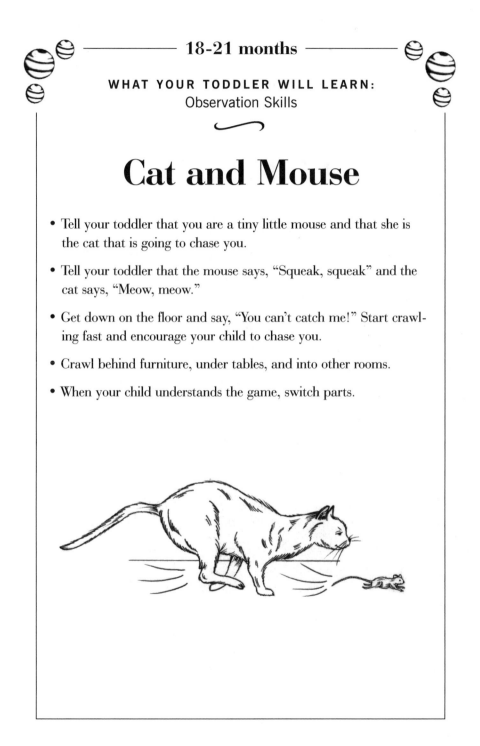

WHAT YOUR TODDLER WILL LEARN:
Spatial Concepts and Creativity

Two Little Blackbirds

- Act out the poem "Two Little Blackbirds."

- Say the words and do the following actions with your toddler. (Change "Jack" and "Jill" to your child's name and one of her friends.)

> *Two little blackbirds sitting on a hill.*
>   *(hold up the index finger of each hand)*
> *One named Jack and one named Jill.*
>   *(move your index fingers in the air and say "tweet, tweet, tweet")*
> *Fly away, Jack.*   *(move one index finger behind back)*
> *Fly away, Jill.*   *(move other index finger behind back)*
> *Come back, Jack.* *(move one finger from behind back)*
> *Come back, Jill.*   *(move second finger from behind back)*

- As you play this game, your toddler may want to "fly" (run) to different parts of the room. What fun!

AUTHOR'S NOTE: I have been playing this game with toddlers for many years, and they absolutely adore it.

Let's Play Train

- Show your toddler pictures of trains. There are many wonderful books about trains.

- Make the sounds that a train makes.
  - Choo, choo
  - Chug, chug
  - Woo, woo
  - All aboard!

- Take four or five chairs and line them up one behind the other.

- Tell your child that she is the engineer and sit her on the first chair.

- Sing songs about trains such as "Down by the Station" and "Little Red Caboose."

- Add the train sounds that you have been practicing to the songs.

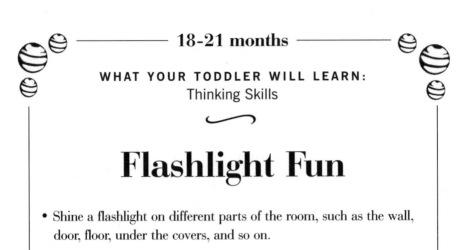

WHAT YOUR TODDLER WILL LEARN:
Thinking Skills

Flashlight Fun

- Shine a flashlight on different parts of the room, such as the wall, door, floor, under the covers, and so on.

- Each time you shine the light on an object, name it. "This is the wall," or "This is the doorknob."

- Show your child how to turn the flashlight on and off.

- Let your toddler shine the flashlight on an object and tell you its name.

- Give your child directions. "Shine the light on the ceiling," or "Shine the light on the window." She may understand what you are saying, even though she might not be able to say the words herself.

- To create a bird shadow on the wall, cross your wrists with your palms facing you. Extend your fingers to make wings and touch the balls of your thumbs together to form the bird's head.

- Move your hands to make the bird "fly."

- Look at pictures in a book or a magazine with the flashlight.

WHAT YOUR TODDLER WILL LEARN:
About Pushing and Pulling

The Push-Pull Game

- Show your toddler how to push a toy car along the floor.

- "Toot, toot, here comes the car." Play pushing cars with your child.

- Tie a string to the car and show her how to pull the car.

- Cut a hole in a box and make a tunnel. Place it on the floor.

- Say to your toddler, "Here comes the car through the tunnel."

- Push the car through the hole.

- Give your child directions to push the car or pull the car.

- Show your toddler how to push things using a cardboard tube from a paper towel roll. Try pushing a ball.

First and Second

- Understanding seriation—first, second, third—is a concept that develops after lots of hands-on play and language experience.

- Sit on the floor with your toddler. Show her a set of nesting measuring cups.

- Take them out one by one. As you take them out, say, "This is the first cup. This is the second cup." With young children, first and second are enough.

- After your child has played with the cups for a few minutes, ask her to give you the first cup. Then ask her to give you the second cup.

- Repeat this game over and over always using the words "first" and "second."

Kitchen Band

- Get out pots, pans, plastic bowls, wooden spoons, metal spoons, and anything else that might make music.

- Sit on the floor with your toddler and start banging the spoons on pots. Hit the pots together, the spoons together, and so on.

- Give a spoon and a pot to your child and encourage her to copy you.

- Chant the following:

> *Pots and pans are fun to play,*
> *Fun to play, fun to play.*
> *Pots and pans are fun to play,*
> *Let's play music.*

WHAT YOUR TODDLER WILL LEARN:
Rhythm

Instrument Fun

- Make two paper bag shakers, one for your child and one for you. Decorate the paper bags with markers and fill them with a little rice or a few dried beans.

- Tie the bags securely and give them to your child.

- Show her how to shake the bags to music.

- Sing favorite songs while you shake the bags.

- Play music of varying tempos and styles, such as marches, waltzes, or any other music that has a distinctive sound.

WHAT YOUR TODDLER WILL LEARN:
About Loud and Soft

Rhythm Fun

- Sit on the floor next to your toddler and give each of you a rhythm stick (or a wooden spoon).

- Show your child how to hit the stick on the floor gently.

- Experiment with your child. Hit the stick loudly and say the word "loud" as you do it. Then try hitting softly and saying the word "soft" as you do it.

- Do the same thing hitting the stick fast and then slowly.

- Once your toddler understands the words and can control the stick, give her directions and see if she can do what you say.
    - Hit your stick fast.
    - Hit your stick slowly.
    - Hit your stick loudly.
    - Hit your stick softly.

- Experiment with hitting the stick on different surfaces, for example, on a carpet and on a floor.

Find the Chair

- Cut out pictures from magazines of objects in your house such as tables, chairs, beds, refrigerator, sink, toilet, and others.

- Show the pictures to your toddler and talk about them.

- Put all of the pictures in a box. Let your child pick out one of them.

- Ask her what is in the picture. If it is a bed, say to her, "Where is your bed?" Take her to a room that has a bed and let her show you the bed.

- Continue naming each picture, finding a matching item in your house.

- Once your child can identify the pictures, make it a little harder by showing pictures of things that are in closets or drawers.

Friends for Breakfast

- Pretending with toddlers is fun for both you and your child. It also develops imagination and creative thinking.

- Invite your child's stuffed animals to breakfast. Sit them around your child and pretend to feed the animals.

- Ask the guests questions such as, "Do you like orange juice?" or "How does the cereal taste?" Answer the questions in different voices.

- Soon you will see your child pretending with her stuffed friends.

WHAT YOUR TODDLER WILL LEARN:
Socialization Skills

Lunch With Teddy

- Tell your toddler that her teddy bear will join you for lunch today.

- While you set a place at the table for teddy, talk about the things that you are doing. "Here is teddy's dish, teddy's cup," and so on.

- Encourage your toddler to ask teddy questions, such as "Will you ask teddy if he likes peanut butter?" This will help your child learn what to say. After your child has asked the questions, ask him, "What did teddy say?"

Napkin Puppets

- Eating out with a toddler is wonderful for developing her social skills.

- Sometimes toddlers get a little fussy and don't want to cooperate.

- Play this game with your child and she will enjoy her restaurant stay.

- Crunch a paper napkin into a round ball. Pretend that it is a puppet and talk to your toddler via the puppet.

- Draw a face on the paper napkin.

- Some things you can say are:
    - "Hello! What would you like to eat?"
    - "I love to drink milk, do you?"
    - "What is your name?"

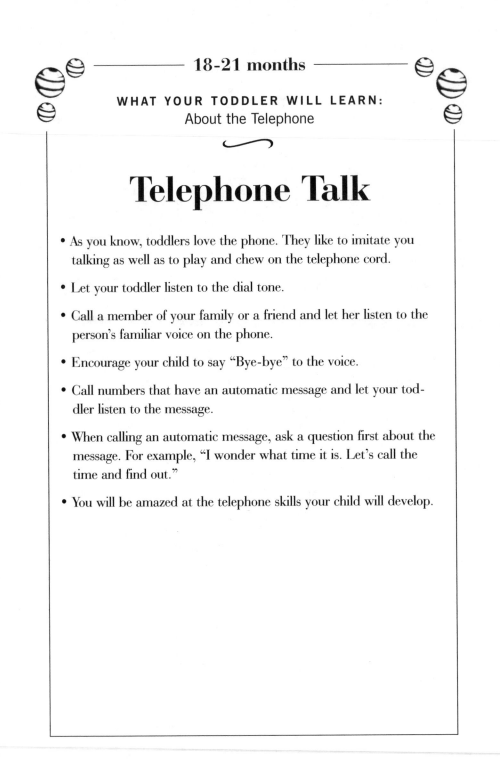

Telephone Talk

- As you know, toddlers love the phone. They like to imitate you talking as well as to play and chew on the telephone cord.

- Let your toddler listen to the dial tone.

- Call a member of your family or a friend and let her listen to the person's familiar voice on the phone.

- Encourage your child to say "Bye-bye" to the voice.

- Call numbers that have an automatic message and let your toddler listen to the message.

- When calling an automatic message, ask a question first about the message. For example, "I wonder what time it is. Let's call the time and find out."

- You will be amazed at the telephone skills your child will develop.

WHAT YOUR TODDLER WILL LEARN:
Language Skills

Car Talk

• This is a good game to occupy your toddler in the car and develop her language at the same time.

• Take a pretend phone in the car with you.

• Ask your child to call the supermarket and ask them if they have any carrots.

• Ask your child to call the library and ask if they have her favorite book.

• Ask your child to call the gas station and ask if they have any gas.

• Give your child different places to call and ask questions about things with which she is familiar.

WHAT YOUR TODDLER WILL LEARN:
Language Skills

Fun With Words

• Nursery rhymes, chants, poems, and songs build literacy.

• Pick two rhymes and say them with your child every day for a week.

• After you have said the rhymes for a couple of days, begin to leave out a word and let your little one fill in the word.

• You can also act out the rhyme, draw pictures of the characters or objects in the rhyme, and say the rhyme in many different kinds of voices.

• After a week, start with two new rhymes. Remember to repeat the familiar rhymes first.

• Rhymes will enhance language development plus give you a lot of fun time with your child.

• Some good rhymes to start with are "Hickory, Dickory, Dock," "Jack Be Nimble," "London Bridge," and "Twinkle, Twinkle, Little Star."

Shoes and Socks

- Undressing your toddler can be a challenge, and it also can be fun.

- Toddlers love to play with their shoes. Loosen the laces and pull the shoe over her heel, so she only has to pull it off the toes.

- Take off socks the same way.

- Encourage your toddler to do as much for herself as she can. As she learns to take off shoes and socks, help her to find words to describe her actions.

Getting Dressed

- When it's time to get dressed, put your toddler's clothes in a pile on the floor.

- Ask your child to bring you the yellow shirt.

- If she brings it to you (chances are that she will), praise her and repeat what she brought to you. "What a good job! You brought the yellow shirt!"

- If she brings you another piece of clothing, say, "Thank you for bringing the blue pants." Help her put on the blue pants, and then ask her again to bring you the yellow shirt.

- Continue asking for each item one at a time. Name the item of clothing and the color.

- When your child can play this game easily, put the clothing in different places in the room and ask, "Bring me the red hat that's on the bed."

- This game is a great self-esteem builder.

WHAT YOUR TODDLER WILL LEARN:
Language Skills

All About Me

- Take photographs of your toddler throughout the day.

- Paste the photographs on heavy paper, punch a hole in each sheet of paper, and attach with metal rings to make a book.

- Look at the pictures with your toddler and talk about the different things that she does during the day: getting dressed, eating, playing, going outside, and taking a bath.

- As you go through the day, show your toddler the picture that relates to each activity.

- You will soon see your child looking at the book and enjoying the pictures.

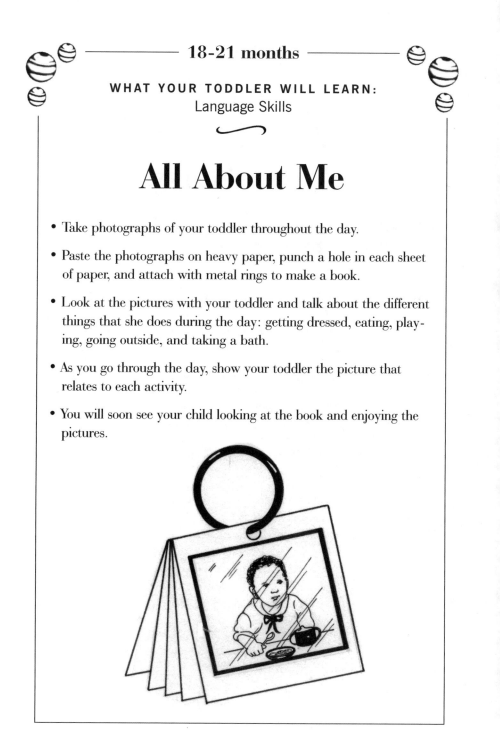

A Box Story

- You will need a square box large enough to glue pictures on all of the sides. Gift boxes work well.

- Cut out pictures of familiar objects from magazines.

- Paste the pictures on the sides of the box.

- Lay down on the floor with your toddler. Touch one side of the box and start telling a story about the pictures on the box.

- Turn the box around and start telling another story.

- This will encourage your child to do the same thing when she is playing. This game really helps your child develop language skills.

- You could also paste pictures from your child's favorite story on the box.

- If you make several of these, they could be stacked as blocks.

WHAT YOUR TODDLER WILL LEARN:
Language Skills

The Mail Is Here

- Before you throw away that junk mail, why not use it to develop your toddler's language skills and coordination?

- Your toddler will enjoy investigating the mail, tearing it, looking at pictures, and examining different shapes and sizes.

- Opening envelopes is great fun for toddlers. If she is unable to, open the envelopes yourself and let her take out the mail.

- The envelopes are full of treasures, such as pictures, and paper with different textures, shapes, and sizes. All of these are stimulating discoveries for your child.

- Pretend to be the mail carrier and say to your child, "The mail is here, and I have some letters for you. Let's see who they are from."

- Pretend to read the letters from Grandma, Uncle Harry, and other family members that your child will recognize.

WHAT YOUR TODDLER WILL LEARN:
A Sense of Family

Photo Albums

- Looking at family pictures is a lovely experience for all ages. Why not start a photo album for your toddler?

- Pick out a special photo album for your toddler and put her name on the front.

- Include in the album a separate picture of each member of your family, including the animals.

- If you are missing a certain person's picture, go visit that person with your child.

- Take pictures together and make it a very special occasion. Then add that picture to the album.

- As your child grows older, she will want to keep adding more pictures, and she will also cherish this album of her family.

Sharing Books

- Although this is in the 18- to 21-month section, reading books to your child is important from birth.

- Remember that toddlers don't sit still very long. Your child may look at a book with you, walk away for awhile, and then come back.

- Toddlers are interested in books about moms and dads, families, going to bed, how things work, animals and babies, sitting on a potty, bugs, and more.

- Look for illustrations that are filled with wonderful information. Talking about the pictures encourages language skills.

- Toddlers like books that are repetitive, rhyme, and are predictable.

- See page 249 for a recommended list of books for toddlers.

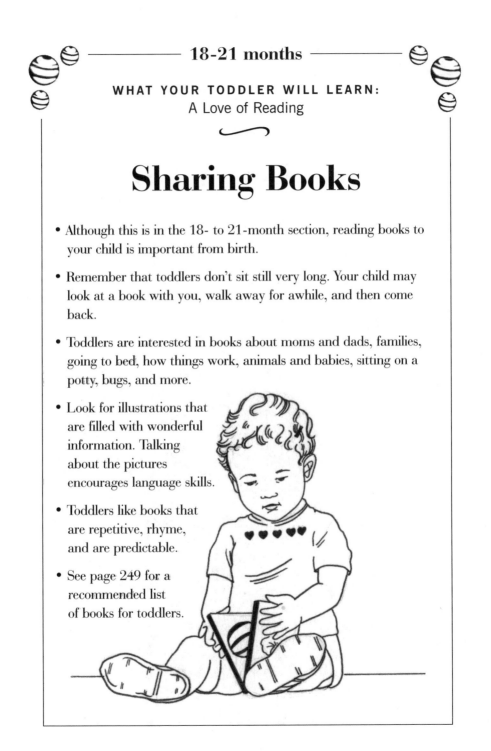

WHAT YOUR TODDLER WILL LEARN:
Imagination

The Sand Game

- A sandbox or sand table is a wonderful toy for young children.

- Many skills can be developed while playing in sand.

- Here are activities to do with sand:
    - Fill and empty cups and containers.
    - Make roads and drive cars over them.
    - Bury your bare feet in the sand.
    - Bury toys and find them.

Colored Water Fun

- This is a good outside or bathtub game.

- Take several see-through plastic jars and fill them with colored water.

- The jars should be small enough that little hands can hold them.

- Show your toddler how to pour the contents of one jar into the other.

- Not only will your toddler gain practice in motor skills, but she will see the color of the water change hues.

Watch the Birds Eat

- Watching birds is fascinating and fun to do with your toddler.

- Make a simple bird feeder using a pinecone. Spread the pinecone with peanut butter, then roll it in birdseed.

- Hang the pinecone near a window where it is easily observed.

- Talk with your child about what birds eat and where they find food.

- You will be amazed at the different birds that come to your feeder. You will have many opportunities to talk about the color, size, language, and other aspects of the birds.

WHAT YOUR TODDLER WILL LEARN:
Coordination

Grasshoppers

- In the summertime, you can usually find grasshoppers outside.

- Show your toddler pictures of grasshoppers.

- Go outside and look for grasshoppers.

- It's great fun to watch grasshoppers hop. Try to imitate the way they hop.

- Pretend to be grasshoppers. Hop around with your toddler.

- Try to make a noise like a grasshopper.

Games to Play with Toddlers

Shadow Play

- Take your toddler outside on a sunny day and show her shadows.

- Walk around the yard or a park and observe the shadows of the trees, buildings, and so on.

- Show her your shadow. Tell her to stand on your shadow.

- Ask her to jump over your shadow. Step on her shadow.

- Draw a chalk line around a shadow cast on a sidewalk.

- Draw a line in the dirt with a stick around a shadow cast in dirt.

Looking for a Rainbow

- There are many ways to play with a garden hose. Try one of the following:
    - Spray the water in a high arc, and let your toddler run under the water.
    - Shoot the water in a stream a few inches off the ground so your child can jump over.
    - Raise the stream and encourage your toddler to crawl under.
    - Wiggle the water back and forth like a snake.
    - Let your toddler water the flowers and grass.
    - Make a mud or sand puddle.
    - Hang the hose over a tree limb or swing set, and let the water run in a steady stream.
    - Look for a rainbow while you spray the water overhead.

- Join in the fun. Let your toddler spray you, too!

WHAT YOUR TODDLER WILL LEARN:
Body Awareness

Foot Fun

- Play this game outside on a nice day.

- Fill a small plastic tub with water and add a very small amount of liquid soap.

- Ask your toddler to take off her shoes and socks all by herself. Tell her that you are going to play a special game with her feet.

- Dip your hand into the soapy water and massage some onto one of her feet.

- As you massage her feet, touch and talk about different parts of the foot: toes, ankle, heel, arch, sole, and skin.

- Dry her foot thoroughly. Repeat the same thing with the other foot.

21-24 months

WHAT YOUR TODDLER WILL LEARN:
Coordination

Baster Game

- This game is a challenge, and your toddler will love squeezing and watching the liquid.

- Arrange two medium-sized plastic bowls next to one another.

- Fill one bowl with water. Add food coloring to the water for artistic purposes.

- Show your toddler how to put the baster into the water and squeeze the bulb. Show him where to look to see the water filling up the tube.

- Show him how to empty the baster into the second bowl.

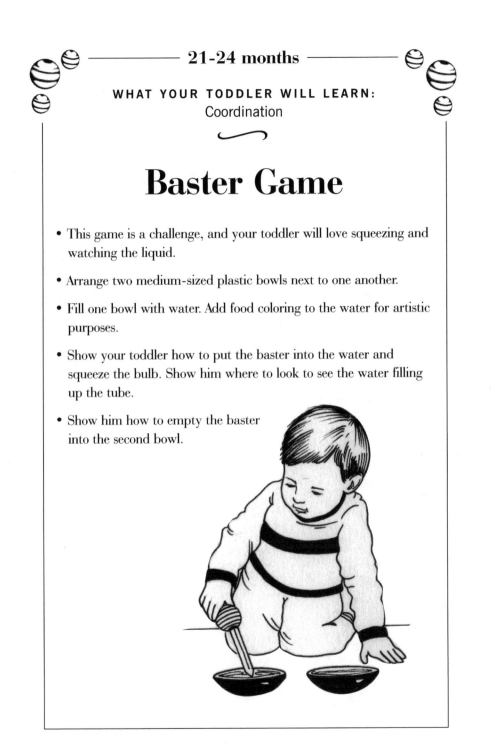

Games to Play with Toddlers

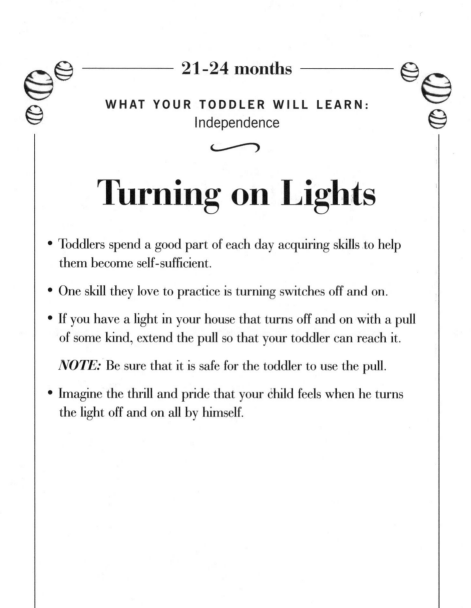

WHAT YOUR TODDLER WILL LEARN:
Independence

Turning on Lights

- Toddlers spend a good part of each day acquiring skills to help them become self-sufficient.

- One skill they love to practice is turning switches off and on.

- If you have a light in your house that turns off and on with a pull of some kind, extend the pull so that your toddler can reach it.

  NOTE: Be sure that it is safe for the toddler to use the pull.

- Imagine the thrill and pride that your child feels when he turns the light off and on all by himself.

WHAT YOUR TODDLER WILL LEARN:
Responsibility

Picking Up the Toys

- Singing is a gentle and pleasant way to accompany a necessary task.

- When your toddler begins to tire of the toys with which he has been playing, invite him to help you pick them up.

- Sit beside him and demonstrate how to pick up a container and drop a toy into it.

- Hand him a toy and ask him to put it into the container.

- Hand another toy to him and ask him to drop it into the container.

- As you continue dropping toys into the container, sing a song that you or your toddler enjoys.

WHAT YOUR TODDLER WILL LEARN:
Observation Skills

Abracadabra

- On large sheets of paper, trace around objects familiar to your child, such as blocks, silverware, a favorite toy, or cookie cutters.

- Put these objects into a box.

- Recite the following "magic words" with your child.

> *Abracadabra, one, two, three,*
> *Look in the box, what do I see?*

- Ask your toddler to pick an object from the box. Help him match it to the outline that you drew.

- The "magic words" makes this game very special. Close your eyes while you say them to make it more fun.

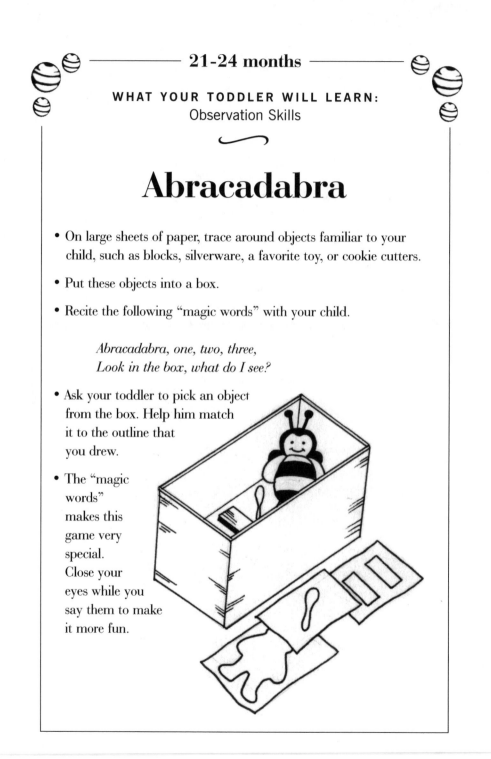

Hand Games

- When a young child plays games that involve his hands and fingers, he exercises the muscles that are so important to later development.

- The following are easy ways for him to play and exercise his hand and finger muscles at the same time.
    - Wiggle your fingers downward like rain falling.
    - Make circles with your fingers and hold them in front of your eyes like binoculars.
    - Move your fingers as if they were paintbrushes.
    - Pound your fist, then clap your hands. Each makes a different sound. Alternate them or create patterns such as pound, clap; pound, pound, clap, clap; pound, clap, clap; and so on.
    - Snap your hands open like popcorn popping.
    - Open and close your thumb and index finger to "snap baby's nose."

WHAT YOUR TODDLER WILL LEARN:
Fine Motor Skills

Where's Your Thumb?

- Show your toddler how to put the thumb of one hand into the fist of his other hand.

- When he can move his thumb in and out of his fist, say the following rhyme.

> *Jack in the box*
> *You sit so still.   (thumb in fist)*
> *Can you come out?*
> *Yes, I will.   (pull thumb out)*

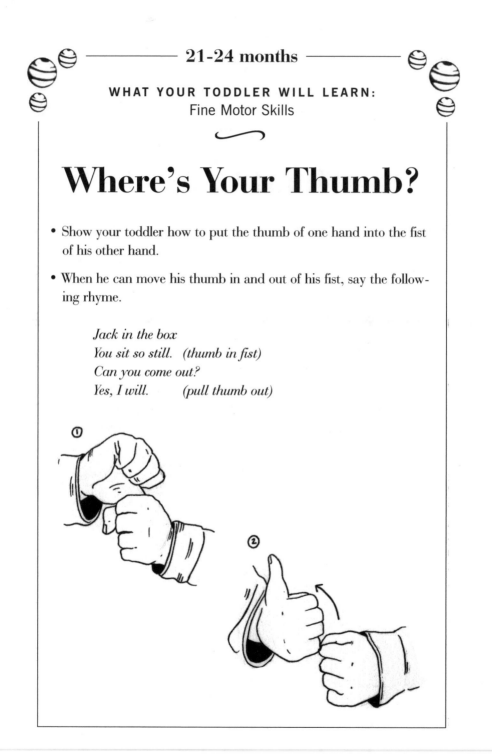

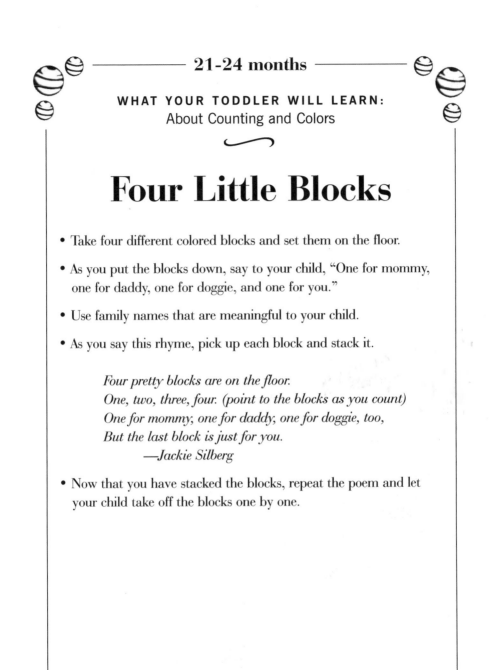

WHAT YOUR TODDLER WILL LEARN:
About Counting and Colors

Four Little Blocks

- Take four different colored blocks and set them on the floor.

- As you put the blocks down, say to your child, "One for mommy, one for daddy, one for doggie, and one for you."

- Use family names that are meaningful to your child.

- As you say this rhyme, pick up each block and stack it.

> *Four pretty blocks are on the floor.*
> *One, two, three, four. (point to the blocks as you count)*
> *One for mommy, one for daddy, one for doggie, too,*
> *But the last block is just for you.*
> *—Jackie Silberg*

- Now that you have stacked the blocks, repeat the poem and let your child take off the blocks one by one.

WHAT YOUR TODDLER WILL LEARN:
Fine Motor Skills

Tu-Be or Not Tu-Be

- Gather different sized cardboard tubes from paper towels, toilet paper, foil, plastic wrap, and any others that you can find.

- Sit on the floor with your toddler and try putting one tube inside the other.

- Encourage your child and praise him when he is able to fit one tube into another.

- Dropping small toys through the tubes is also great fun, but supervise this closely so he does not put small things into his mouth.

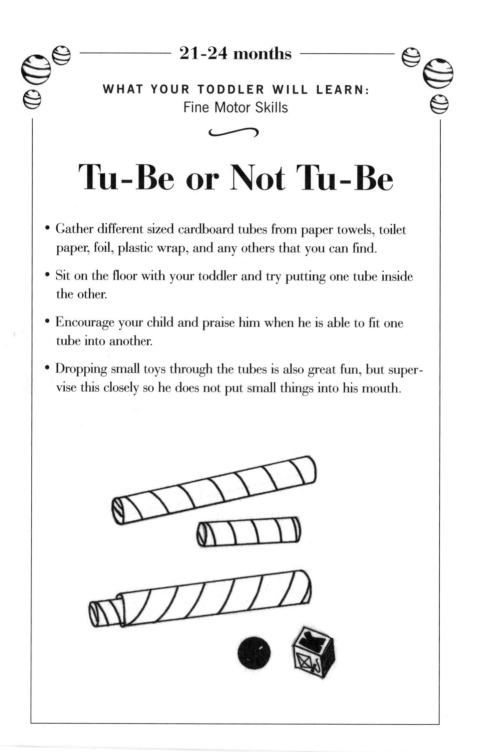

Collage

- Gather together lots of odds and ends—paper, junk mail, greeting cards, pieces of Styrofoam, string, yarn, wrapping paper, beans, and other collage materials.

  NOTE: Supervise closely as toddlers may still put things into their mouths.

- Lay a large sheet of heavy paper or cardboard on the table.

- Using a glue stick, dab glue on one thing at a time and give it to your child to place on the paper.

- Or, let him select the things he wants you to glue.

- Your child can dab on the glue as long as he is closely supervised.

- Hang the finished collage in a prominent place for everyone to admire.

WHAT YOUR TODDLER WILL LEARN:
Fine Motor Skills

Sticky Fun

- This game takes a little work on the part of the adult, but you will find that it is worth it when you see the joy your toddler will experience.

- Make a sticky board by putting clear self-adhesive paper over heavy cardboard. The cardboard should be about the size of a place mat.

- Take the backing off of the paper so that the sticky part is facing up.

- Then take additional adhesive paper and attach the sticky paper to the cardboard, then frame it along all four sides.

- Have precut pictures from magazines that your child can pick up and stick on the paper.

- A fall theme of pictures might be trees, squirrels, or apples. Select pictures appropriate to the season.

- This is a game your toddler will want to play many, many times.

WHAT YOUR TODDLER WILL LEARN:
Creativity

Snow Pictures

- This game should be played when you can see snow on the ground.

- Give your toddler white paper and let him tear it into small pieces.

- Take a piece of blue construction paper and place it on a table.

- Put some glue on a piece of the paper and let your toddler place the "snowflakes" on the blue paper.

- When the picture is finished, hang it on the wall for all to see.

WHAT YOUR TODDLER WILL LEARN:
Creativity

Working With Clay

- The following are activities for you and your toddler to try with modeling clay.
    - Help your child make balls and snakes.
    - Talk about the colors of the clay. Mix the colors together.
    - Form shapes with clay such as circles, triangles, and squares.
    - Make letters.
    - Press or roll the clay with a rolling pin. Make patterns on the flattened surface with blocks, toys, a comb, or rocks.
    - Cut the clay with cookie cutters.

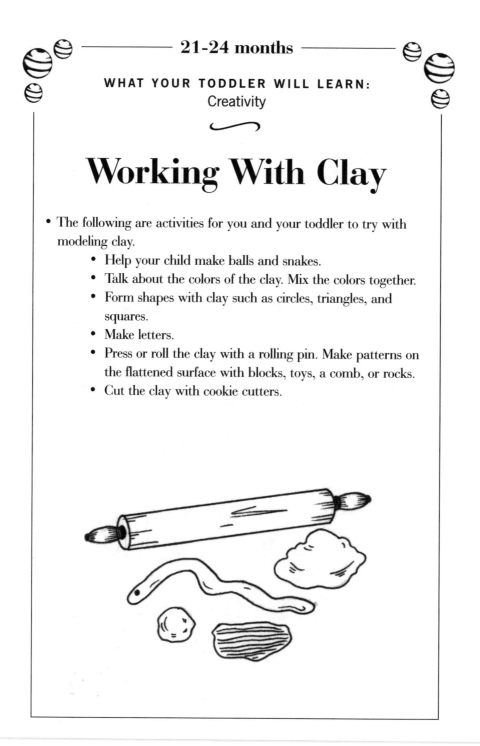

The Sticker Game

- Toddlers love stickers! Make a special card to send to a friend, to grandparents, or to each other.

- Select stickers that have the same shape. Geometric shapes will help children learn about shapes.

- Print something simple on a sheet of 8½ in. x 11 in. paper. For example, "Dear Grandpa, I love you."

- Tell your child what the words say, then let him decorate the paper with stickers. You may have to show him how to lift the stickers off the paper and put the stickers on the paper.

- When you are finished, mail it to the special person.

The Sound Game

- Put into several film canisters things that make a variety of sounds, such as a coin, a button, a cotton ball, popcorn, or sand.

  NOTE: Be sure that the canister lids are fastened securely and that your toddler cannot remove them.

- Show your toddler how to shake the canisters. Give him time to shake them and listen to all the sounds.

- Pick two canisters, one that makes a loud sound and the other, a soft sound. Shake the soft one and say, "Soft...shhh," in a very soft voice. Shake the louder one and say, in a loud voice, "Loud."

- Ask your toddler to shake the soft one and then the loud one.

- As he holds the canisters, he will become aware that one is heavier, and one is lighter. Although he is too young to understand this concept, he is acquiring a feel for differences in weight.

- Try using the words "noisy" and "quiet" instead of soft and loud.

WHAT YOUR TODDLER WILL LEARN:
A Sense of Rhythm

Drumbeats

- You will need some drum music to play on a cassette or CD.

- Show your child all the different ways that he can make drum-beats or move to the rhythm of the music.
    - Hit your fists on different surfaces.
    - Use wooden spoons or rhythm sticks to play on different surfaces.
    - Sit on the floor and bounce your bottom to the rhythm.
    - Play imaginary drumsticks in the air.
    - Shake your entire body to the rhythm of the music.

- Rhythm experiences help young children learn listening skills and coordination.

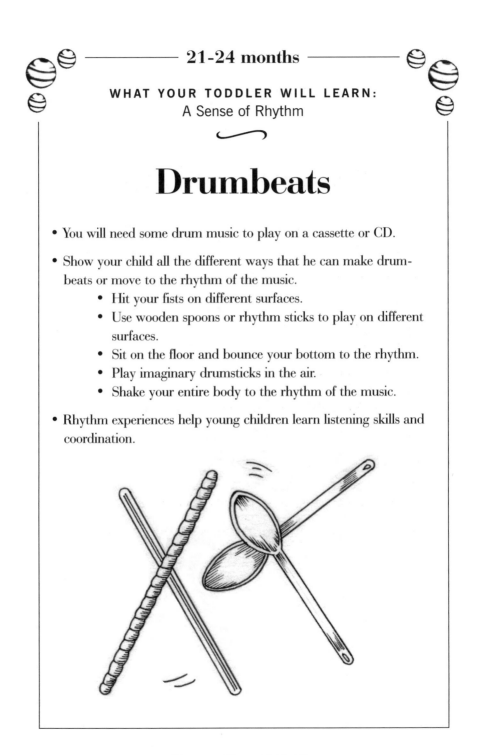

Winding Up the Clock

• Show your toddler a wind-up clock.

• Show him how you can wind it up on the back. You could also use a stuffed animal that has a wind-up part.

• Let your toddler listen to the "tick tock" of the clock.

• Imitate the sound and say the words "tick tock."

Instruments Make Music

- Creating simple rhythm instruments will thrill your toddler and make singing more fun.

- Drums can be made from a round box. Cover the open end with adhesive-backed plastic. Put a rubber band over the plastic around the rim to be sure that it is secure. The smaller the box, the higher pitched the sound; the larger the box, the lower the sound.

- Make shakers by putting rocks, beads or buttons inside film containers. Securely fasten the lids.

- Play your instruments while you sing a favorite song.

Up and Down

- Play games with a small xylophone.

- Let your toddler experiment with hitting the tones. This takes fine motor skills to hit the mallet on the tone bar.

- Take the mallet and hit each tone from low to high. Sing the scale as you do this.

- Now hit the notes and sing the scale downward.

- Crouch down with your hands on the floor. Sing the scale again as you move your body upward and stretch your hands high in the sky.

- Now come back down as you sing the scale downward.

- Don't be surprised to find your child trying to do the same thing in the near future.

Marching

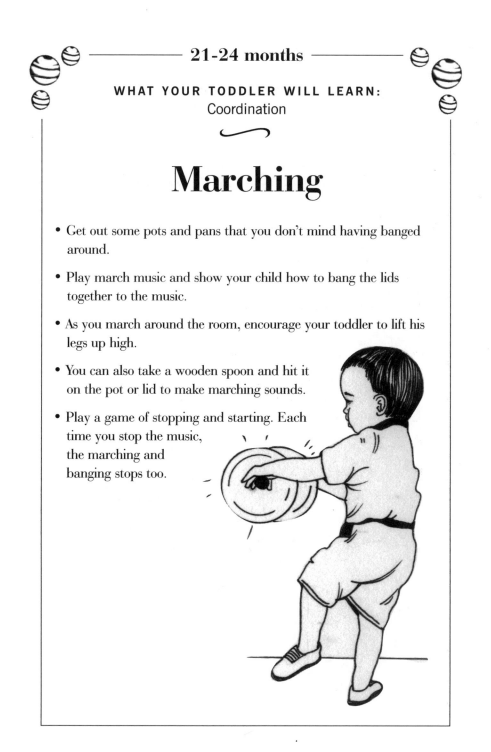

- Get out some pots and pans that you don't mind having banged around.

- Play march music and show your child how to bang the lids together to the music.

- As you march around the room, encourage your toddler to lift his legs up high.

- You can also take a wooden spoon and hit it on the pot or lid to make marching sounds.

- Play a game of stopping and starting. Each time you stop the music, the marching and banging stops too.

WHAT YOUR TODDLER WILL LEARN:
Imagination and Fun

Let's Have a Parade!

- Gather a few of your toddler's toys, cars, trucks, dolls, and other toys. Line them up in a straight line.

- If you can fit some of the toys on top of the cars, that makes it even more fun.

- Play some march music and pretend to have a parade by moving the different toys to the music.

- Show your toddler how to march and the two of you can march to the music.

- If you have a drum handy, hit the drum as you march.

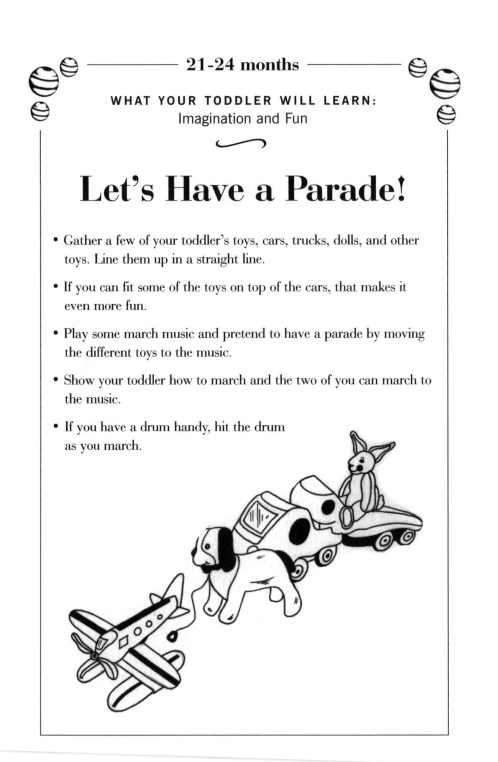

WHAT YOUR TODDLER WILL LEARN:
Listening Skills

Tape Recorders

- Toddlers love to have their own tape players. There are many tape recorders that are very simple to use.

- Make up a story using your child's name in the story. Tell the story on tape so that your child can listen to it over and over.

- Listening to a parent's voice is very calming to a young toddler.

- Select a variety of tapes for your child. Classical, children's songs, pop tunes, and a variety of musical styles.

Twos

- Toddlers are not ready to count or recognize numbers, but they can understand the basic concept of "two."

- Help your child begin to understand this concept by pointing out many things that come in pairs.
    - two shoes
    - two socks
    - two hands
    - two feet
    - two ears

- In your daily conversation, use the word "two" whenever possible. "Look at these two flowers."

- Give your toddler things in "twos." "Here are two spoons," or "Here are two toys."

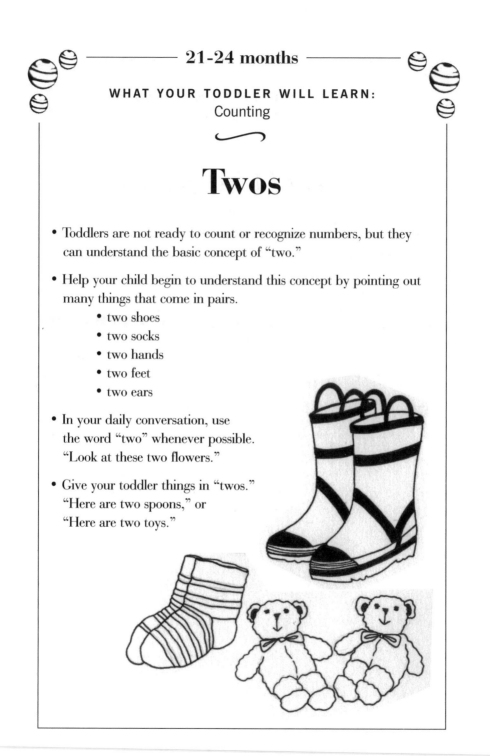

You Choose

- Toddlers enjoy choosing between two objects. This gives them a wonderful sense of power.

- Sit on the floor with your child facing you.

- Put two favorite toys in front of him.

- Hold up one toy and talk about it. Describe the color, what it can do, the size, and any other things that you think would be important to your child.

- Pick up the second toy and describe it as well.

- Ask your child to select one of the toys and give it to you.

- Praise his choice.

- Ask your toddler to put the toy in another place. Give him two choices—on the table or on the chair.

WHAT YOUR TODDLER WILL LEARN:
About Colors

Mixing Colors

- Talk about colors with your toddler. If you have a book about colors, read it to him.

- Take one of the three basic colors (red, yellow, or blue) and walk around your house pointing out that color to your child.

- It's best to point out one color at a time.

- Play this game with another color on another day.

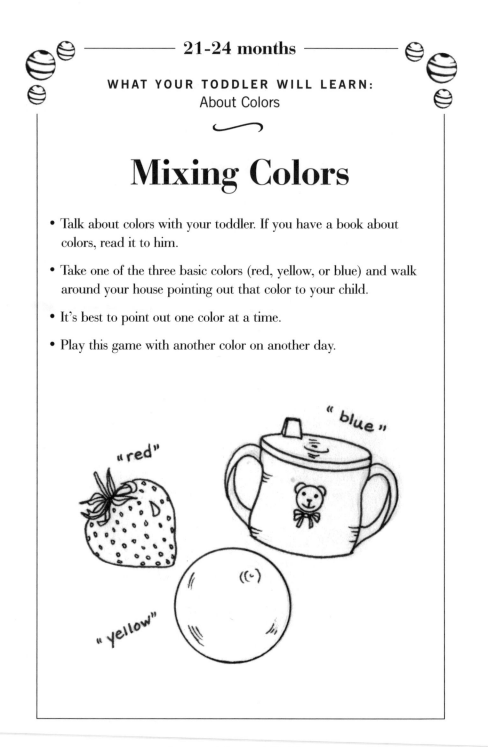

"red"

"blue"

"yellow"

Blue Circle

- Cut out circles, squares, or triangles of two different colors. Start with blue, yellow, or red.

- Lay the cut-out shapes on a table in front of you and your toddler.

- Start with the blue circle.

- Pick it up and place it in front of you.

- As you move the circle, say, "Blue circle."

- Pick up a second blue circle and say, "Blue circle."

- Point to each circle and say, "One, two, I love you."

- After you have done this a few times, ask your child if he knows where a blue circle is.

- Another day, try this game with triangles or squares.

Spots and Stripes

• Find pieces of material or articles of clothing that have spots and stripes on them.

• Show your toddler the spots. Touch them, count them, or trace your finger around them. Let him become familiar with the shape and the name.

• Do the same with the striped material.

• Draw spots and stripes on paper and let your child tell you which are the spots and which are the stripes.

• Walk around the house and look for spots and stripes. Many times, you will find them on walls or floors as well as canned goods.

• Look at an animal picture book. Find animals with spots or stripes.

WHAT YOUR TODDLER WILL LEARN:
About the Senses

Sensory Experiences

- Your toddler loves to explore. Encourage him by taking his hand and touching many things. Materials of silk, wool, cotton, and corduroy are a wonderful variety of textures.

- Help him compare how things feel by saying things such as, "This feels smooth and this feels silky."

- Nature provides wonderful smells (flowers, grass, leaves) as well as crunchy leaves to touch and soft grass to walk on.

- The kitchen is full of wonderful tastes—sweet, sour, spicy, and more!

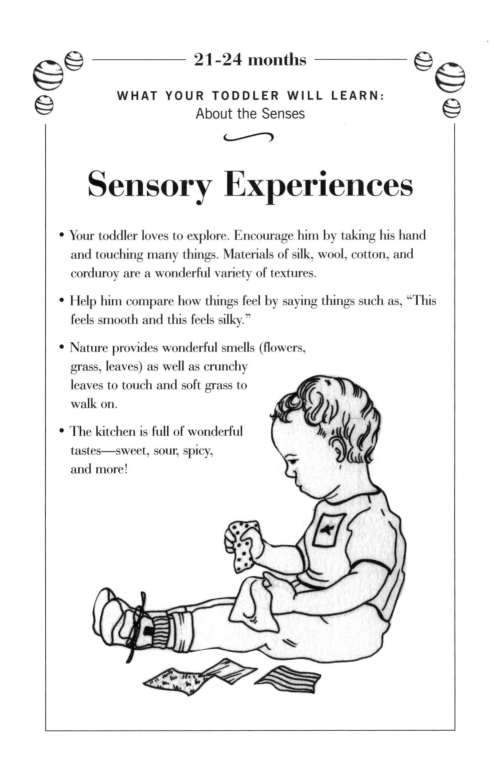

To the Supermarket

- A trip to the supermarket is a rich, educational experience for a toddler.

- Plan a trip that is short so that your little one will not tire out.

- Pick four or five items that have different textures.

- As you put each one into the cart, let your toddler touch and feel the item.

- Talk about each item and how it feels. Is it smooth, soft, cool, hard, bumpy, or another texture?

- Suggestions include:
  - Cereal boxes
  - Small cans
  - Small plastic bottles
  - Fruits or vegetables with unique textures, such as avocados, oranges, or kiwis

- The supermarket is an exciting world of sights, sounds, and touch.

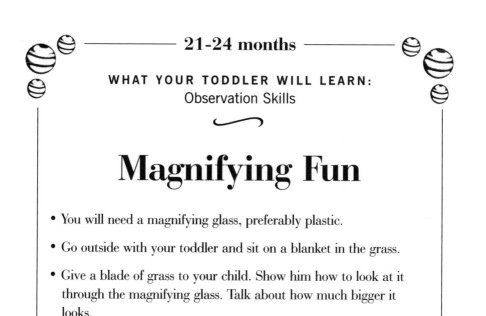

WHAT YOUR TODDLER WILL LEARN:
Observation Skills

Magnifying Fun

- You will need a magnifying glass, preferably plastic.

- Go outside with your toddler and sit on a blanket in the grass.

- Give a blade of grass to your child. Show him how to look at it through the magnifying glass. Talk about how much bigger it looks.

- Help your child examine his body with the magnifying glass. Fingernails, skin—especially something with a Band-Aid on it— and toenails are fascinating.

- Walk around the yard and see what you can find. Look at a leaf, and under a leaf. Examine a flower or the bark of a tree.

- Get on the ground and see if you can find any crawling things.

- Your child will probably want to carry the magnifying glass around all the time. If he does, make sure it is a plastic one.

Spinning Around

- Cut pictures from magazines of things familiar to your toddler—animals, people, toys, and other familiar objects.

- Get a lazy Susan tray or something similar that spins around.

- Lay the pictures on the tray—you may have to tape them down—and spin it.

- While you spin the tray, say, "One, two, three, spin."

- When the tray stops, point to the picture in front of your child and talk to him about it.

- Continue playing the game. If the same picture stops in front of your toddler, talk about it again.

- Let your child try to spin the tray.

- This kind of interaction will build your child's vocabulary and help create a special relationship between you and him.

WHAT YOUR TODDLER WILL LEARN:
Language Skills

First Reading Game

- Cut pictures out of catalogs and magazines. Paste the pictures onto cards.

- Show a picture to your toddler and talk to him about it. Talk about the color, the shape, how it is used, and so on.

- Give the card to your toddler and name the object, for example, "shoe."

- Ask your toddler to give you the "shoe" picture.

- Once he understands, introduce another picture card. Then, when you ask him for a picture, he will have to choose between two.

Double Fun

- This game takes a lot of concentration for your toddler and will develop his thinking skills.

- Cut out a magazine picture of something your child recognizes, for example, a piece of fruit.

- If you cut out a picture of a banana, put it on the floor in front of your toddler.

- Say, "Look at this picture of a banana. Yum, yum."

- Talk about the picture with your child.

- Now, get a real banana and put it next to the picture.

- Talk about the real banana in the same way that you talked about the picture.

- Continue playing this game of matching the magazine picture to the real thing.

- Cut out several familiar objects and ask your child to take the picture and put it on the real object.

- For example, "Can you take this picture of the pillow and put it on the pillow?"

What's Next?

- Select a favorite book that your child enjoys reading.

- As you read the book talk about what's on the next page before you actually turn the page.

- When you turn the page, point out what you were talking about. For example, "Here is the little boy who fell asleep in the haystack."

- Each time you turn the page, try to give your child something to anticipate on the following page. In no time, he will be telling you what is on the next page.

- Let your child turn the book pages. This is excellent for developing fine motor skills.

WHAT YOUR TODDLER WILL LEARN:
Thinking Skills

Peekaboo Book

- Get a spiral notebook that opens like a book (5 in. x 8 in. is a good size).

- Glue pictures of familiar objects to every other page. If the book were open in front of you, the pictures would be glued to the right-hand page.

- Cut the page without any picture into several wide horizontal strips, starting with the left edge of the paper and cutting within two inches of the spiral.

- This enables your toddler to cover the picture on the right with the strips. Look at the book with your toddler. Turn over one strip at a time, gradually revealing more of the picture. Ask your child to guess what the picture is.

Cut the page with no picture into wide horizontal strips.

Feelings

- Find pictures of people expressing feelings of happiness, sadness, laughter, crying, and other emotions. Magazines are a good source.

- Paste the pictures on cardboard squares. Punch holes in each square and tie them together with ribbon to make a special book to share with your toddler.

- Look at the pictures with your child and talk about each one. For example:
    - If you see someone laughing, laugh out loud and encourage your child to do the same. Talk about why the person might be laughing.
    - If you see someone crying, pretend to cry and encourage your toddler to do that, too. Talk about why the person might be crying.

- It is important that young children feel free to express their feelings.

- Your toddler will soon look at this book by himself.

WHAT YOUR TODDLER WILL LEARN:
Self-Esteem

Making Gifts

- Talk with your toddler about making a gift for another person.

- Decide who it will be, perhaps a grandparent, another relative, the child's friend, or a neighbor.

- Go through magazines and choose pictures that the recipient of the gift might like or that the toddler likes.

- Cut out the pictures for your toddler and help him paste them on a paper plate.

- Let him choose where to put the pictures on the plate.

- Help him give the paper plate to someone of his choosing.

- Your child will learn about doing things for others and will also practice using his imagination, learning about shapes, sizes and colors, and feel proud of himself.

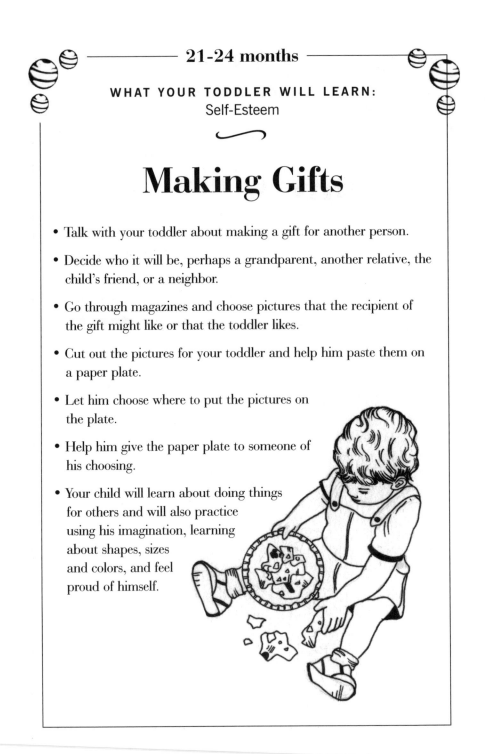

Driving Teddy

- Ask your toddler to "drive the car." Show him how to move his arms from left to right as he turns the make-believe steering wheel.

- Walk around the room pretending that you are driving the car.

- Once your toddler can do this, ask him to let his teddy bear drive the car.

- Show him how to move teddy's arms.

- As you walk around the room driving the car, make car sounds. Pretend to beep the horn, and put your foot on the brake when you stop.

The Swimming Doll

• Get a rubber doll with moveable arms and feet, if possible.

• Encourage your toddler to teach the doll to swim.

• Show him how to move the doll's arms and legs.

• Give him directions on ways to move the doll in the water, for example, splashing, kicking, or floating.

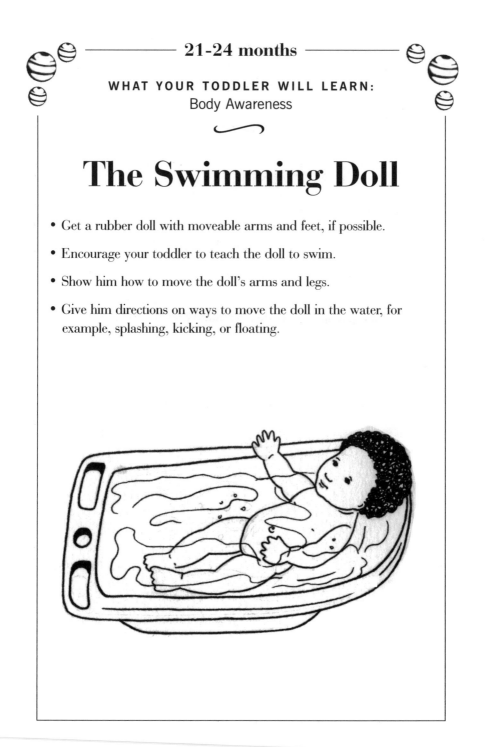

WHAT YOUR TODDLER WILL LEARN:
Language Skills

Telephone Time

- Car phones are so popular these days that a toy phone in the car seems natural.

- While your toddler sits in his car seat, suggest he call someone.

- Tell him where you are going and ask him to call ahead. "Call Grandma and tell her that we will be there soon." Give him an idea of what to say: "Hello, Grandma, we'll be there in five minutes."

- Whether you are going to the supermarket, to the park, or to pick up someone from school, pretend to call them from the car.

- After a few times, your child will have his own ideas of what to say.

WHAT YOUR TODDLER WILL LEARN:
Observation Skills

Lookie, Lookie

- Make a toy from the cardboard tube of a paper towel roll.

- Show your toddler how to look through the tube.

- Ask the child to find a certain object. When he finds it, ask him to say, "Lookie, lookie, I see a _____." For example:
    Adult: "Can you find something red?"
    Child: "Lookie, lookie, I see a red _____."
    Adult: "Can you find something tall?"
    Child: "Lookie, lookie, I see a tall_____."

- Toddlers love to say, "Lookie, lookie." (Maybe because it sounds like "cookie.")

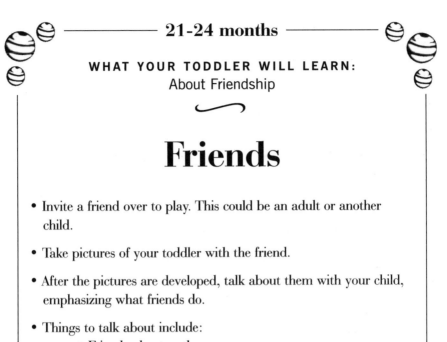

Friends

- Invite a friend over to play. This could be an adult or another child.

- Take pictures of your toddler with the friend.

- After the pictures are developed, talk about them with your child, emphasizing what friends do.

- Things to talk about include:
  - Friends play together.
  - Friends take turns playing with toys.
  - Friends laugh with you.
  - Friends give you hugs.
  - Friends like to be with you.

I Brush My Teeth

- This is a game to teach your toddler about taking care of himself.

- Say the following poem.

    I brush my teeth in the morning,
    I brush my teeth in the morning,
    I brush my teeth in the morning,
    Every single day.

- Recite the poem while pretending to brush your teeth. Help your toddler pretend to brush his teeth.

- Try these additional verses, reciting and miming the actions.

    I comb my hair....
    I wash my face....
    I wash my hands....
    I drink my milk....

- Make up your own verses about the things that you do each day.

WHAT YOUR TODDLER WILL LEARN:
Vocabulary

Copy Cat Language

- Your toddler is beginning to talk and experiment with sounds.

- You can expand on everything your toddler says by adding words to his words.

- When he says the word "milk," you can say, "Yes, this is cool, white milk."

- Each time he says a word, repeat the word and add descriptive words about it, expanding his words into a short sentence.

- This is a wonderful way to encourage language development.

WHAT YOUR TODDLER WILL LEARN:
Self-Confidence

Undressing

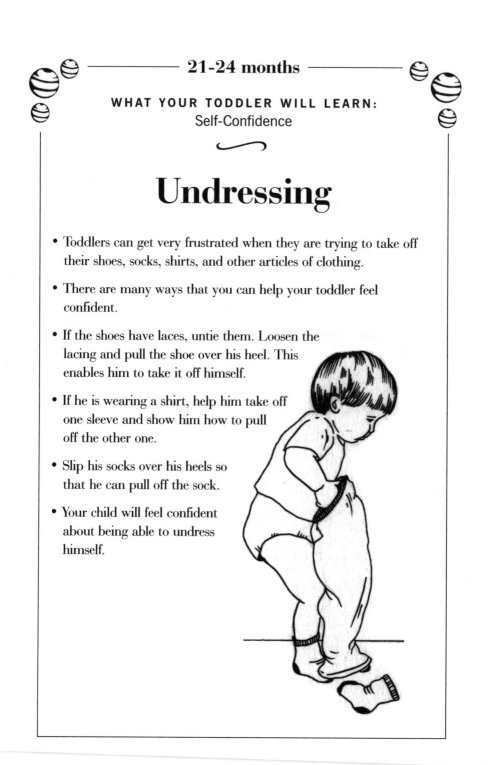

- Toddlers can get very frustrated when they are trying to take off their shoes, socks, shirts, and other articles of clothing.

- There are many ways that you can help your toddler feel confident.

- If the shoes have laces, untie them. Loosen the lacing and pull the shoe over his heel. This enables him to take it off himself.

- If he is wearing a shirt, help him take off one sleeve and show him how to pull off the other one.

- Slip his socks over his heels so that he can pull off the sock.

- Your child will feel confident about being able to undress himself.

Walking Games

- Once your toddler has learned to walk, there are many activities to increase his coordination.

- Show him how to walk different ways, such as sideways, backward, or high-legged like a horse.

- March, walk on tiptoe, or slide your feet.

- Hang your arms in front of you, your hands clasped and swaying back and forth. Walk slowly as you swing your "elephant trunk."

- Walk slowly and walk fast.

- Encourage your child to hop, jump, skip, and run.

- Walk while talking in different voices—a low voice, a high voice, a baby voice, and so on.

WHAT YOUR TODDLER WILL LEARN:
Responsibility

Cleaning Up

- Toddlers often protest when you want to wipe their face and hands when they are finished eating.

- Take a wet cloth and show your child how you wipe your face and hands.

- Give a wet cloth to your child and ask him to wipe his face and hands.

- When the meal is finished, give your toddler a sponge or wet cloth to wipe the table.

- Toddlers love to please you, so give him a lot of praise.

Footprints in the Snow

- When the ground is covered with snow, it is fascinating to walk outside and study footprints.

- Take your toddler outside and look for prints in the snow. Try to figure out what bird or animal made those footprints.

- Let your toddler put his hand in the snow and look at his hand-print.

- Put your hand in the snow and compare your print with your toddler's print.

- Compare your shoe or boot prints to your toddler's.

- This is a game that I still like to play even though my children are grown.

WHAT YOUR TODDLER WILL LEARN:
Coordination

Can You Tell Me?

- This game helps toddlers associate the language that goes with motor skills.

- Say to your toddler, "Can you tell me what I am doing?"

- Jump up and down a few times. Then say, "I am jumping."

- Now say to your child, "Can you jump like me?"

- Help your child jump up and down.

- Repeat this activity with several motor skills. Marching, swimming (use your arms), and running are all good ones.

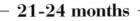

Follow the Leader

- Make a straight path on the floor with newspapers, taping them into place.

- Show the path to your toddler and say, "This is the long path you can walk on."

- Demonstrate how to walk on the path using both arms to balance.

- Ask your toddler to follow you on the path. If he doesn't understand, hold his hand to guide him. If you have to help your child, you will need another person to lead.

- If your toddler is able to follow the first path, make a more difficult path that curves or winds in and out of other rooms.

AUTHOR'S NOTE: This is a game the entire family can play.

WHAT YOUR TODDLER WILL LEARN:
About Shapes

Walking on Shapes

- Use wide, sturdy tape to create shapes on the floor, such as circles, squares, triangles, and zigzags.

- Show your toddler how to walk on the tape. Start with the circle.

- Hold your toddler's hand and walk together.

- After you have walked on all the shapes, try other ways to move across them: walk backwards, sideways, on your tiptoes. Try to hop, jump, crawl, and march on the shapes.

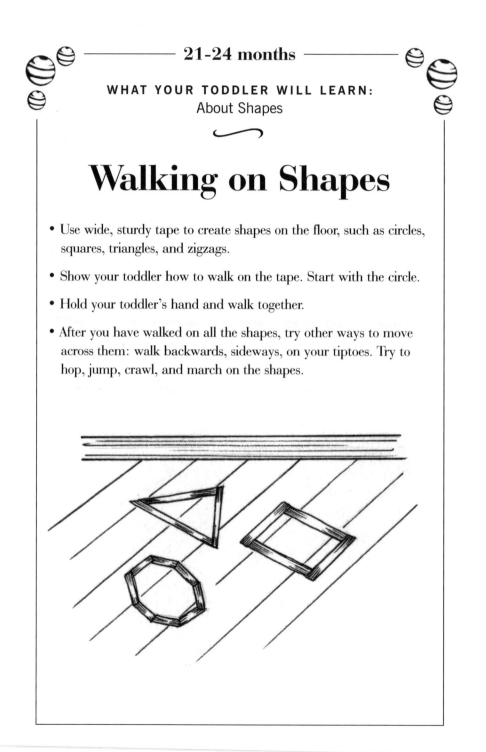

WHAT YOUR TODDLER WILL LEARN:
Gross Motor Skills

Run to the Tree

- Toddlers love to run. This game will give your toddler an opportunity to run and improve his language skills.

- Walk around the yard with your toddler. Tie colorful ribbons in two or three places—a tree, a door, a familiar area.

- Say to your toddler, "I'm going to run to the tree." Holding his hand, run to the tree. Run to the other places, each time telling him where you're going.

- Next, ask your toddler to run to the tree, the door, or wherever you are. He will adore this, especially if you praise him when he reaches his destination.

Jumping Game

- This wonderful game requires strength, balance, coordination, and agility.

- Find a box strong enough to support your toddler's weight. Set your toddler on the box and take both of his hands in yours.

- "Ready, set, GO!" Help him jump off the box. Your arms should be at his shoulder height so that he lands on his own weight.

- He will love this and want to do it again and again.

Where Can I Jump?

- Toddlers can run and jump forever. Provide many opportunities for your child to exercise his muscles.

- Place barriers for your child to jump over. Start with something low and raise it higher. Blocks are good barriers for jumping.

- If your child has some trouble, help him by lifting him at the waist.

- Make a circle with masking tape and show your toddler how to jump in and out of the circle.

- Outside, encourage your child to jump off curbs and over water puddles.

- Pretend to be a kangaroo and jump everywhere.

Jumpin' Teddy Bear

- Spread a large towel on the floor.

- Place your child's teddy bear in the middle of the towel. Tell your child that the teddy bear is going to jump.

- Ask your toddler to hold one end of the towel while you hold the other, saying, "One, two, wheee!" Lift the towel into the air.

- Practice so that your toddler will understand whenever he hears "wheee," to lift up the towel.

- The idea is to keep the teddy bear on the towel.

- After a few times, move the towel faster in order to toss the teddy bear higher in the air.

- Tossing and trying to catch the bear in the towel takes a lot of eye-hand coordination.

- When the bear drops, let him scoop it up and put it back into the towel.

- This is a lot of fun. Your toddler will want to put other things into the blanket besides the ball.

WHAT YOUR TODDLER WILL LEARN:
Coordination

Spring Movements

- Play this game outside on a lovely spring day.

- Pick two or three movements that you can do with your child, for example, walking, running, and jumping.

- Tell your toddler that you are going to walk to the tree. Holding your child's hand, walk to a tree and stop.

- Next, tell your toddler that you are going to run to the door. Holding your child's hand, run to the door.

- Continue running, walking, or jumping to a designated spot.

Games to Play with Toddlers

WHAT YOUR TODDLER WILL LEARN:
Language Skills

Bubbly Fun

- Fill a large bowl with water and place it on a table outside.

- Take a straw and blow gently on your child's hand.

- Show him how to take the straw and blow gently in the water. Tip: Some children will need additional practice blowing OUT and not IN. To prevent children from sucking up the water if they inhale, cut a v-shaped slit in the straw (about three inches from the top of the straw).

- Call his attention to the bubbles in the water.

- Once he gets the idea, he will figure out that the harder he blows out, the more bubbles he will have.

- Blowing is an important developmental skill for speech. The letters, "p," "b," and "w" are all formed with a blowing motion.

- You can add detergent to the water for big, blowy bubbles if you desire. *NOTE:* Add detergent only when your toddler understands that he should only blow OUT and not IN.

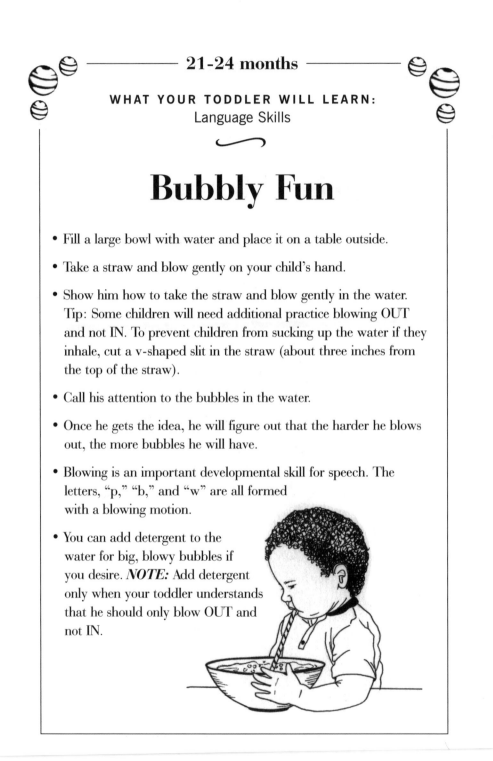

Sand Play

- Making designs in the sand can be wonderfully creative. Your little artist will get much pleasure from playing with sand.

- In your kitchen drawers you will find many utensils that make interesting designs in the sand: pancake turner, slotted spoon, measuring cups, pizza cutter, zester, and cookie cutters, to name a few.

- Show your toddler how to put each utensil into the sand to make a design.

- Show your toddler how to fill a cup with sand, then turn it over to make a hill.

- Make a hole in the sand and stick a utensil into it.

- Demonstrating these tools to your toddler will inspire him to create his own designs.

- An enjoyable indoor version of this game is to fill a large baking pan with salt. Make designs in the salt. To erase, just shake the pan.

WHAT YOUR TODDLER WILL LEARN:
Coordination

Roll the Ball

- Sit on the grass facing your toddler.

- Sit far enough apart that you can roll a ball to your toddler, and he can catch it easily.

- Encourage your child to roll the ball back to you.

- As your toddler gets better at doing this, make the rolling space wider between the two of you.

- Roll the ball to a tree or other outside place.

- Ask your toddler to bring it back to you or run with your toddler to get the ball.

Playing Catch

- A partially deflated beach ball is an excellent ball for a beginner because it is easy to grasp.

- Another adult should stand about three feet from your child to throw the ball.

- Stand behind your toddler and guide his hands through the first few catches and tosses.

- Show your toddler how to make a cradle with his arms to catch the ball.

- Ask the other player to toss the ball.

- Play catch!

WHAT YOUR TODDLER WILL LEARN:
Coordination

Bowling

- Turn three or four paper cups upside down on the floor.

- Take a small ball and show your child how to roll the ball and knock down the cups.

- Each time that a cup is knocked down, clap your hands and shout, "Hooray!"

- Encourage your child to try knocking down the cups. Have him sit close enough to the cups that he will be successful in knocking them down.

- After your toddler has learned to do this well, you can set up groups of cups in several places in the room, and let him try to knock down all of them.

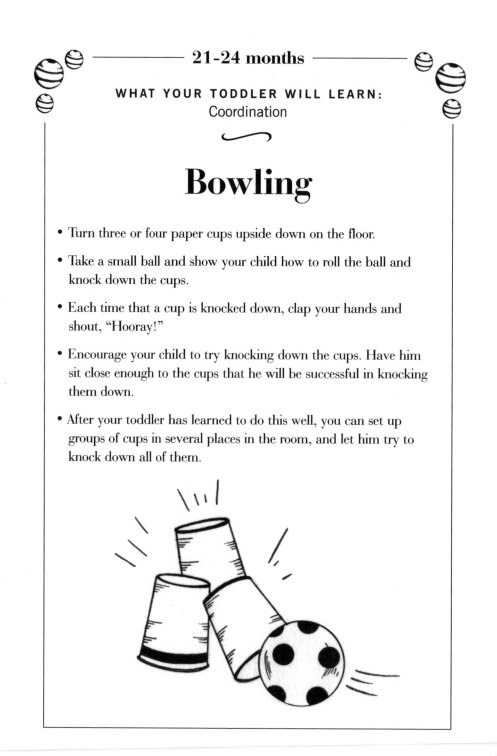

Recommended Books for Toddlers

Barnyard Dance! by Sandra Boynton
The Bear Went Over the Mountain by Rosemary Wells
Brown Bear, Brown Bear, What Do You See? by Bill Martin, Jr.
Clap Your Hands by Lorinda Bryan Cauley
Families by Debbie Bailey
Have You Seen My Duckling? by Nancy Tafuri
Here Are My Hands by Bill Martin, Jr. and John Archambault, illustrated
   by Ted Rand
Hey! Wake Up! by Sandra Boynton
I Went Walking by Sue Williams
If You Were My Bunny by Kate McMillan
Jesse Bear, What Will You Wear? by Nancy White Carlstrom and
   illustrated by Bruce Degan
More! by Sheilagh Noble
My First Songs collected and illustrated by Jane Mannin
On Mother's Lap by Ann Hebert Scott
On My Street by Eve Merriam, illustrations by Melanie Hope Greenberg
Pots and Pans by Patricia Hubbell
Roll Over! A Counting Song, illustrated by Merle Peek
Skip to My Lou adapted and illustrated by Nadine Bernard Westcott
Ten, Nine, Eight by Molly Bang
This Is the Farmer by Nancy Tafuri
Tomie's Little Mother Goose by Tomie dePaola
Uh Oh! by Sheilagh Noble
Whoops! by Louise Batchelor

Index

Games to Play with Toddlers

ABOUT THE AUTHOR

Photo © 2015 Trevor Williams

Andrew Case is a seasoned playwright and author of the stage plays *The Electric Century, Pacific, The Rant,* and many others. He has been a member of the New American Writers Group at Primary Stages, a participating playwright at the Eugene O'Neill Theatre Center, and a member of the PEN America Center.

For nearly a decade, he served as an investigator, spokesman, and policy director at the Civilian Complaint Review Board, which investigates allegations of misconduct against New York City Police Department officers. His scholarship on police oversight has appeared in the *Columbia Human Rights Law Review.*

Andrew lives in Flatbush, Brooklyn, with his wife, Claudia, and their two children. *The Big Fear* is his first novel.